Brilliant Buil̲ PC

Geoff Spick

Harlow, England • London • New York • Boston • San Francisco • Toronto • Sydney • Singapore • Hong Kong
Tokyo • Seoul • Taipei • New Delhi • Cape Town • Madrid • Mexico City • Amsterdam • Munich • Paris • Milan

Pearson Education Limited
Edinburgh Gate
Harlow
Essex CM20 2JE
England

and Associated Companies throughout the world

Visit us on the World Wide Web at:
www.pearsoned.co.uk

First published 2007

ISBN-13: 978-0-13-204878-1
ISBN-10: 0-13-204878-7

British Library Cataloguing-in-Publication Data
A catalogue record for this book is available from the British Library

Library of Congress Cataloging-in-Publication Data
A catalog record for this book is available from the Library of Congress

10 9 8 7 6 5 4 3 2 1
10 09 08 07 06

Prepared for Pearson Education Ltd by Syllaba Ltd (http://www.syllaba.co.uk).
Typeset in 12pt Arial Condensed by 30
Printed and bound in Great Britain by Ashford Colour Press Ltd, Gosport.

The publisher's policy is to use paper manufactured from sustainable forests.

Brilliant guides

What you need to know and how to do it

When you're working on your PC and come up against a problem that you're unsure how to solve, or want to accomplish something in an application that you aren't sure how to do, where do you look? Manuals and traditional training guides are usually too big and unwieldy and are intended to be used as end-to-end training resources, making it hard to get to the info you need right away without having to wade through pages of background information that you just don't need at that moment – and helplines are rarely that helpful!

Brilliant guides have been developed to allow you to find the info you need easily and without fuss and guide you through the task using a highly visual, step-by-step approach – providing exactly what you need to know when you need it!

Brilliant guides provide the quick easy-to-access information that you need, using a detailed table of contents and troubleshooting guide to help you find exactly what you need to know, and then presenting each task in a visual manner. Numbered steps guide you through each task or problem, using numerous screenshots to illustrate each step. Added features include 'See also' boxes that point you to related tasks and information in the book, while 'Did you know?' sections alert you to relevant expert tips, tricks and advice to further expand your skills and knowledge.

In addition to covering all major office PC applications, and related computing subjects, the *Brilliant* series also contains titles that will help you in every aspect of your working life, such as writing the perfect CV, answering the toughest interview questions and moving on in your career.

Brilliant guides are the light at the end of the tunnel when you are faced with any minor or major task.

Author's acknowledgements

For my family: you're all brilliant!

Publisher's acknowledgements

The author and publisher would like to thank the following for permission to reproduce material in this book:

AOpen Inc, ASRock Inc, Adobe Systems Inc, Advanced Micro Devices Inc, Apple Computer Inc, Arctic Cooling GmbH Corsair Memory, Creative Technology Ltd, ENlight Corporation, Futuremark Corporation, Grisoft, Google, Intel Corporation, Kingston Technology Company, LG Electronics, MSI Computer Corporation, MajorGeeks.com, NVIDIA Corporation, OpenOffice.org, Opera Software, Plextor Corp, Qualcomm Inc, Sapphire Inc, STOPzilla, USRobotics, Western Digital Corporation, WinZip International LLC.

Microsoft product screenshots reprinted with permission from Microsoft Corporation.

In some instances we have been unable to trace the owners of copyright material, and we would appreciate any information that would enable us to do so.

Photography by Simon Muncer – www.simonmuncer.co.uk

Special thanks to Matt Powell for permission to use material on pages 9–18 which first appeared in his book 'Brilliant Computer Basics'.

About the author

Since 1994 when the Internet was a realm of enthusiasts waiting to explode, Geoff Spick has written for, and edited, PC and technology magazines. These include Internet Today, CD-ROM User, NetGamer, Strategy Player, PC First Aid and PC Home and Web Designer.

Contents

Introduction

Welcome to *Brilliant Build your own PC*, an annotated visual guide that explains all you need to know about selecting the right parts and putting them all together to create your own customized PC. From start to finish it gives you all you'll require to make the smart choice, stick to a budget and get the right result.

Find what you need to know – when you need it

Everything from getting the right parts for your own PC given the huge range of makes, models and different standards, to how to assemble all the parts together into a working PC, to how to test and optimize your newly built system is covered here.

You don't have to read this book in any particular order. We've designed the book so that you can jump in, get the information you need, and jump out. To find the information that you need, just look up the task in the table of contents or Troubleshooting guide, and turn to the page listed. Read the task introduction, follow the step-by-step instructions along with the illustration, and you're done.

How this book works

Once you've got all the parts, actually building a PC is the work of just a few hours. With the handy step-by-step guide you'll be shown where everything goes. Each task is presented with step-by-step instructions in one column and annotated screen illustrations in the other. This arrangement lets you focus on a single task without having to turn the pages too often.

Step-by-step instructions

This book provides concise step-by-step instructions that show you how to accomplish a task. Each set of instructions includes illustrations that directly correspond to the easy-to-read steps. Eye-catching text features provide additional helpful information in bite-sized chunks to help you work more efficiently or to teach you more in-depth information. The 'For your information' feature provides tips and techniques to help you work smarter, while the 'See also' cross-references lead you to other parts of the book containing related information about the task. Essential information is highlighted in 'Important' boxes that will ensure you don't miss any vital suggestions and advice.

Troubleshooting guide

The PC is a technical marvel but can be prone to all kinds of problems during setup. Very few of them are serious but even trivial issues can have obscure solutions. They are explained here.

The Troubleshooting guide offers quick and easy ways to diagnose and solve common problems that you might encounter. The problems are grouped into categories that are presented alphabetically.

Spelling

We have used UK spelling conventions throughout this book. You may therefore notice some inconsistencies between the text and the software on your computer which is likely to have been developed in the USA. We have however adopted US spelling for the words 'disk' and 'program' as these are becoming commonly accepted throughout the world.

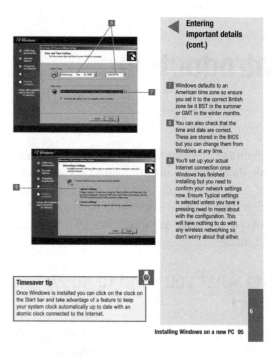

Entering important details (cont.)

7. Windows defaults to an American time zone so ensure you set it to the correct British zone be it BST in the summer or GMT in the winter months.

8. You can also check that the time and date are correct. These are stored in the BIOS but you can change them from Windows at any time.

9. You'll set up your actual Internet connection once Windows has finished installing but you need to confirm your network settings now. Ensure Typical settings is selected unless you have a pressing need to mess about with the configuration. This will have nothing to do with any wireless networking so don't worry about that either.

Timesaver tip

Once Windows is installed you can click on the clock on the Start bar and take advantage of a feature to keep your system clock automatically up to date with an atomic clock connected to the Internet.

Installing Windows on a new PC 95

Troubleshooting guide

Only a decade ago, getting computer parts required a trip to a specialist store. Now, however, almost every high-street store has a selection and the once-oppressive PC stores who catered only for the experts of old now cater for the humble shopper on the street. In the better chain stores, staff members are trained to understand the capabilities of what it is they're selling, while a local retailer should really know his business and be able to offer practical advice.

The Internet has changed the way many of us shop and computer stores were one of the first natural areas of online shopping. A host of massive web stores sell huge ranges of gear at prices that the high street cannot match. Of course there are the postal system and returns policies to worry about but the savings on offer are causing more and more of us to shop this way.

Another angle you can check out is the joy of eBay and other online auction houses. You can find major bargains on even the latest kit if you're prepared to venture into one of these. With brand new, nearly new and second-hand gear out there from the millions of users of a growing number of auction sites, the choice is vast.

Do you want it right now?

If simplicity and speed are the keys for you then your best option is to march into a local computer store, be it an independent or chain

> **Jargon buster**
>
> **eBay** – the first online selling and buying site, eBay allows millions of us to put up for online auction, or sale at a fixed price, our unwanted possessions. eBay is so successful, that many small businesses have started up selling PC parts and peripherals online, often far cheaper than you will find on the high street.

store, present your list and get all the parts on the spot. If you have to take a step up or, less likely, down the performance ladder on one part then it might not make much difference to the price. However, don't let anyone bully you into buying more than you need.

If the store doesn't have one particular part, ask when they can get it in stock. Make sure you get a definite answer before deciding if it's worth the wait. If you don't want to wait then find out if there's anywhere else locally where you can get it at a similar price. Having a backup plan before you set out is always a good idea.

If you have time to spend before making a buying decision, do all the browsing you can. Prices of computer parts change by the day, and prices between stores and sites can vary by a few percent. If you happen upon a sale, then you can be quids in on decent gear at excellent prices.

Buying the parts (cont.)

How to buy online

If you choose to buy your system online, you'll be either pleased or boggled by the massive amount of choice there is. From huge superstores to local shops with a net presence, there's a sizeable range. Also, prices on a web site can change on a daily basis. If you want to go down this route then decide on a few sites you feel confident buying from; you might be happier choosing a big name brand or just one that has an online stock system where you can see exactly what's sitting on the shelves in their warehouse.

What you might want to do at this point is create a spreadsheet listing the components you're interested in. Have a column for each shop to tally the prices and, of course, check that VAT is added to the prices. Leave a row for postage costs. Once you've found the best deal then make your order. We've included a chart you can use at the end of this chapter.

For your information

Processor prices come down in big chunks whenever Intel or AMD releases a new chip. Keep an eye on technology news sites like www.theregister.co.uk for details of any new launch or imminent price cuts to make sure you bag a bargain. The recent introduction of Dual-core chips, effectively two processors in one, means that single core chips are becoming as cheap as, um…, chips.

Jargon buster

Dual-core – in an attempt to speed up computers in the past, motherboard makers put two processor slots on a single board. This was expensive and required lots of extra wiring. To cheapen the idea of doubling your power, Intel and AMD are both putting two, and now four, processor cores on a single chip, saving the motherboard makers doing any extra work. With two processors working together, tasks take less time and more work can be done between the cores.

Filling in a system-specification sheet

Please make a copy of this page and use it when planning what system to buy. You can compare costs from different stores and of different types of systems. If you have a firm idea of what you want then you can get straight on with filling it out. If you're not sure what to get then fill it in as you decide while reading on through these chapters. You can also tick off components as you purchase them if you're buying from a range of sources.

See also

The next 10 pages will give you a quick overview of the kinds of components you'll be buying.

	AMD system	Intel system	Preferred retailer	2nd retailer
Case				
Processor type				
Motherboard				
RAM quantity				
Graphics card				
Audio card				
Hard drive size				
Optical drive				
Extras				

Motherboard

Think of the motherboard as your PC's central nervous system. Its job is to connect and manage each component, shuttling data to the correct location. Not all motherboards are the same and the type of hardware you can use is restricted by what will physically fit on the board and what is supported by the motherboard chipset.

Central Processing Unit

Continuing the biological analogy, the central processing unit (usually referred to as the CPU or processor) is the brain of any system. It does the hard work of calculating all the data it's given by the motherboard. The power of a CPU is measured in GHz (older CPUs under 1 GHz were measured in MHz) but, increasingly, manufacturers are leaving off the GHz speed in marketing materials as it becomes less important. Processors run extremely hot, requiring heatsinks and powerful fans to cool them.

Random Access Memory (RAM), or just memory, is extremely fast volatile memory that provides temporary data storage when a computer is in use. Volatile memory loses the data held when there's no power. The more RAM you have, the faster your system will operate as

it's able to shunt data there while getting on with other tasks and retrieve it when needed. RAM often comes in pairs, but since there are many different kinds of RAM these must be of the same type and, preferably, from the same manufacturer.

Hard disk drive

The hard disk, hard drive or HDD is the main storage medium for modern computer systems. While RAM is volatile, hard disks are non-volatile so data written to them is kept until manually deleted. Current consumer level hard disks have reached 500 gigabytes (GB) in capacity. There are several types of interface for hard disks, the most common being IDE and SATA.

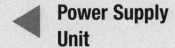

Power Supply Unit

The Power Supply Unit (PSU) regulates and distributes power to your PC. Its output, measured in watts, is important as this limits how much hardware you can fit before your system's power requirements exceed the capability of the PSU. For most of us, a good quality 350 W PSU is perfectly adequate.

PC case ▶

Usually referred to as the case, enclosure, or chassis, this metal or plastic box is what holds all your components together. Cases vary in price and complexity from sub-£20 plastic models to high-tech aluminium costing many hundreds of pounds. If you have a choice it is worth looking at your options, since airflow, build quality and features can be important depending on your needs. If you're running a system with expensive high-end graphics cards and hard disks you'll need to ensure that there's a constant flow of cool air. You may also want extras such as tool-less operation (which allows you to open the case and remove components without a screwdriver) or accessible front-mounted interface ports.

Choosing your hardware

2

Introduction

Choosing what bits of kit to buy is the technology equivalent of being let loose in a sweet shop as a child. The choice of PC parts is substantially wider than that of the pick-'n'-mix bins so it is important to keep two key objectives in mind when choosing your kit: ensure compatibility between all items and try to get the most power and performance for your budget.

Choosing your case

The PC survived for around 20 years in nothing more alluring than a beige metal or plastic rectangular box, but that all changed when home users and gamers started demanding something a little sexier. At first it was the addition of some svelte contours and a subtle range of colours to make the case distinct from the humble office system. Now, as customisers and artists get creative with what you cram the pieces of a computer into, you can get cases that look like they've come off the battlefield, from the future, or from the bottom of a skip.

Your cheap, traditional, standard PC case is a light plastic affair that will cost little more than £20-30 and fulfil all the needs of the typical PC user. It might even come with a power supply already installed, saving some money straight away. Even cheaper cases have a little styling to them and maybe some Perspex windows so you can see inside.

There are three sizes of basic case: the larger, called a full tower, offers more space for hard disks and CD or DVD drives and, handily, more room in which to operate when upgrading your system; the micro tower is the smallest basic case and just has room for one or two DVD drives in a very cramped space; finally, the midi tower is the most common type of case and takes the middle ground with plenty of space and room to upgrade.

Then came small windows in the side, LED lighting in the case and a mass of tricked-out gadgets to make cheap and fun modifications possible for all. More recently, very expensive cases made with costly metals or custom parts add to today's more radical designs.

In recent years, the idea of the PC as a home entertainment centre has seen designs emerge which try to fit in with your current DVD player and television and make use of wireless peripherals to prevent a tangle of leads ruining the effect. This effort has continued with the quest for smaller PCs and quieter systems, the ultimate being the Mac Mini, a computer no bigger than a lunchbox, and which several PC companies have tried to emulate. Whatever your desire, you'll be spoilt for choice with PC cases, just remember that all these extras cost you money and the smaller the case the less you'll be able to fit inside or upgrade.

What to consider before choosing a case

Where will it go? Often, larger cases are kept under a desk so as not to eat into your workspace. If it's out of sight there's no need for any pretty extras.

Do you want form over function? With varying degrees of stylish cases do you just want a regular case that looks nice or are you going all out to make a statement? The choice will have a big impact on your budget

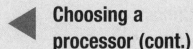

retail package will contain everything you need to run the chip to the PC's motherboard. OEM versions are cheaper because they have none of these parts (such as cooling) and no fancy packaging.

2

Jargon buster

OEM – this stands for Other End Manufacturer and refers to a computer part that is sold to commercial builders to be put into their own machines that are sold complete under their own brand name. Lots of these parts, from processors to graphics cards, end up for public sale cheaper than the retail versions. The drawback is that often the warranty is shorter than that of the retail product and the part comes with none of the frills that you'd find in a retail box. So there's no fancy packaging, no extra software and the minimum of documentation.

For your information

What you get – when you buy a processor you generally get the chip and its cooling system in one package. Not so, though, with the OEM models as mentioned earlier. If you do go the OEM route then you'll need your own cooler and, to keep your chip running as chilled as possible, you may want to invest in a higher quality fan and cooler paste than you would normally get.

Choosing a motherboard

Now that you've decided which processor to buy, you can select a motherboard to run it on. The processor you've chosen will have a pin-count number, 754, 755, 939 or some other figure. All you need to do is make sure your motherboard has the same number; they are generally referred to by the same code. The only other limitation is if you're going for a small form factor case; this will limit you to the tiny Micro-ATX motherboards.

For each type of processor there is a huge range of motherboards suited to all budgets from the cost-conscious buyer to the power business user. Dozens of features are listed on the front of each motherboard box, and the reality of exactly how complex computers are can hit you right here.

Usually, on the front of the case the model name will be in big letters with the pin number prominently listed. Then you'll see a number of different features listed in nicely coloured boxes. When buying the rest of your components you need to make sure they match the standards listed. So if the box states that the motherboard will handle DDRII 667 and DDR 400 RAM then you can choose components that run on either of those. Budget-conscious fans will be pleased to hear that they can buy the cheaper RAM initially and then replace it with the speedier RAM when they decide to upgrade.

A similar decision needs to be made about the support for video cards. Most new motherboards support PXI Express graphics cards while some budget cards support only the older, slower AGP standard. A few boards will support both, allowing for further flexibility in your buying and upgrading path.

Other boxes that you might want ticked are support for SATA hard drives, which can read data faster than traditional IDE drives, and RAID support, which lets you create automatic backups of your data using two or more hard disks.

You can pick up motherboards from between £50 and £150. The higher the cost the more features you'll find on the board. Some high-end specialist boards allow for multiple processors, more memory banks, or high-end features that you might otherwise have to buy separately.

Other features, such as surround sound, seem to come as standard on most boards and are accepted as the norm. The balance you need to strike is getting all the features you can on a board without going over the top on price. Competition is fierce and the main name brands, ASUS, MSI and others all do decent ranges to cover most budgets.

Jargon buster

RAID – Redundant Array of Inexpensive Drives is a fancy way of saying that if you install two or more hard drives in your PC then you can back up your data between them. Therefore, if one file becomes corrupted you will always have a backup on one of the other drives. RAID does this automatically, so you need never worry about corrupt files again.

For your information

Save the Earth – environmental factors might not rate highly in your buying process but look out for a new logo called RoHS on motherboards and other computer products. This means they were built in accordance with the Restriction of Hazardous Substances directive from the European Union, an act that bans the use of hazardous chemicals in the production of electrical equipment.

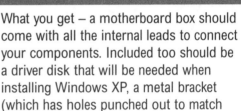

For your information

What you get – a motherboard box should come with all the internal leads to connect your components. Included too should be a driver disk that will be needed when installing Windows XP, a metal bracket (which has holes punched out to match the outputs of the board) to be fitted on the case, and a manual that explains all the features (they are generally light on details of actually installing the board).

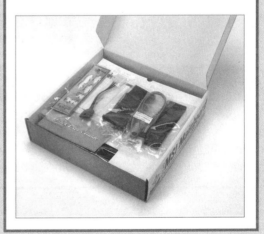

Getting a graphics card

Your motherboard purchase will help you decide if you need to go for an accelerated graphics port (AGP) or a peripheral component interconnect (PCI) graphics card. The only choice left is how much to spend, as these cards range from between £30 and £400 pounds. The cheapest cards come with little of their own memory and will borrow some of your system RAM to do their processing. As a budget solution it is fine but it slows down graphics performance, something that won't be of benefit if you want games or video power.

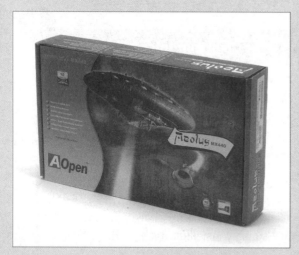

The highest-end cards have all the latest features and up to 512 MB of their own memory. Mid-range cards have some features turned off and average 128 MB of RAM. It's fairly clear what you'll get from a particular card but the rule is really that only hardcore gamers need to spend more than £150 on a video card, everyone else will get on fine with something at or below that limit; it just depends how far your budget will stretch.

For your information

What you get – a graphics card generally comes with only a driver CD and, if you're lucky some demo games to play. Some will come with a video adapter that will let you plug old-style D-pin monitors into the newer type connectors. Cards with TV and other features will have a breakout box that lets you connect a range of video inputs.

little use until traditional DVD has run its course. Their one advantage is massive storage, up to 50 GB of data crammed on to a single disk, but for now most of us will be happy with the 5-10 GB offered by standard DVDs.

Different disk standards

Of course you can't get through this section without a warning about a couple of hitches. There are so many DVD standards that it's almost painful. Every time a new standard comes out

most DVD-writing software needs an update but, in reality, it's a small pain. The most recent dual-layer feature lets us burn 9.7 GB of data to a disk.

As for the two behemoth next-generation standards, no one really knows if there will be a winner before 2008 or if they'll co-exist forever. What is a fact is that the early drives will be priced ridiculously high and there's no real need for a PC owner to buy one unless you specifically want to watch high definition movies on your PC.

2

For your information

The LightScribe version of the humble disk burner uses a special foil in the disk, and the laser as a fine 'pencil', to burn the label text or picture directly into the disk. This is a charming niche feature that you might want to splash out on to make presentation disks but it has little practical value for most of us.

Considering other essentials

There are quite a few other bits and bobs that could easily be overlooked but which are still required purchases for your shiny PC. These might be cheap and not the most glamorous aspects of your system but could prove vital in getting it to run!

Floppy drive

You can run a PC quite happily without a floppy drive and you'll rarely see a floppy disk in a commercial package. However, there are particular situations where one might be invaluable or even essential. While building a recent PC with a SATA hard drive, the Windows XP installer required the use of a floppy drive in order to read the SATA driver file; without one we could go no further. Since they cost around £5 and only take a minute extra to install, it's not really wasting a lot of money and you'd be surprised how many people still use those little plastic disks to store and move files around despite the rise in popularity of USB memory cards.

Display

We're going on the basis that you're going to plug your new system into your existing monitor. As one of the more expensive parts of a system, it's what most people keep when they go to upgrade. However, if you want a new one then we can heartily recommend the huge range of flat-screen LCD displays that dominate the market.

Prices have crashed in the last couple of years and now it's probably harder to even find an old chunky style monitor. LCDs take up a lot less space than do their predecessors, are quieter in operation and consume less power. Of course, more and more users are plugging their systems into the TV for gaming and watching movies.

2

Keyboard and mouse

Your old input devices might be looking a bit
tatty by now but the good news is that perfectly
usable replacements can be had for around £10.
If you want to go a little up market then you can
invest in wireless kit that removes a couple of
those nagging desktop wires but is likely to add
to your battery bill. Many keyboards offer extra
media function buttons but in reality 99% of
users ignore them and so will you.

First steps in building your PC

Introduction

So you've got all those shiny boxes of bits offering untold power once they're all put together. We recommend you don't rattle them like Christmas presents to see what's inside! You're now eager to get on with building your system. All you need is a decent amount of desk space, a couple of hours of free time and no interruptions or interference from children or pets. For safety's sake, keep any drinks well out of reach; coffee-stained processors don't work as well for some reason. For preference, work in plenty of light. If you can't, then angle-poise lamps are excellent for helping you peer into the case. Aside from the computer parts, you'll also want an anti-static wrist strap and, ideally, a computer toolkit. In reality, though, you can build the whole system with just a Philips-head screwdriver.

Important !

Before unpacking anything from its packaging make sure your anti-static strap is being worn and is connected to a suitable ground source (this has to be some unpainted metal connected to an earthed source, be it a central-heating pipe or something similar). If you haven't got anything to hand then follow the first steps of this chapter and connect it to the case once the power supply is installed. This will prevent the build-up in your body of any destructive static.

What you'll do

Install the power supply

Unpack the components

Install the processor

Add the cooling

Install an AMD processor

Install an Intel processor

For your information

You'll need the following equipment and components for this chapter:

Earthing strip

Philips screwdriver or PC kit

Processor

Motherboard

Memory

Case

Power supply

Installing the power supply

To install your power supply, get the PSU and the case out of their boxes. If the PSU is supplied already fitted in the case then you've no worries. Just plug the power supply into the mains, making sure that both power switches, on the wall and the PSU, are switched off. Connect your wrist strap to a bare bit of metal on the case.

If you need to install the power supply then follow the steps below and begin the journey into building your own PC.

1 Examine the power supply and the space for it on the case. In almost all systems the power supply sits at the top to keep the hot air it generates away from the main components. To fit the power supply, align the unit's screw holes with those on the case. They are laid out in a standard manner and will only line up one way. Metal supports or guides inside the case will take the weight of the power supply when you slot it in.

Timesaver tip

You might want to plug the power supply into the mains and see if it works before bolting it into the computer. The fans should spin and any lights it has will function. It is extremely unlikely that there will be a problem with it, but it's good to be sure before going to the trouble of bolting it into the case.

Installing the power supply (cont.)

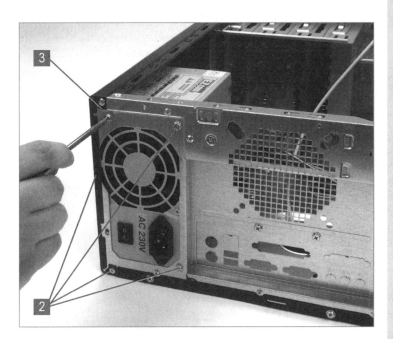

2 Once that's done you can slide the supply box fully into the case until the screw holes are aligned. Now use the screws provided to lock it into place. Fix all four screws in place with a few turns until you're sure everything fits securely.

3 Once you're happy, tighten up all the screws. Don't over-tighten them but make sure the power supply is securely fitted as a loose one will cause lots of unwanted vibration within the case. Inside the case you may find a hook near the supply. Hang the wire loom on this to partially prevent the wires flopping about inside the case.

3

! Important

The screws for the PSU will come as part of the motherboard bundle. There are several sizes, a couple of which will do the job. It's a case of stating the obvious but if they don't fit, then don't force them. Use a consistent type and ensure they can hold the PSU tightly.

For your information

Some of the newer, luxury power supplies come with modular cabling, so you only need to plug into the supply those cables you actually require. They are more expensive than the basic models but useful if you want a clutter-free case.

Installing the power supply (cont.)

4 Connect the power cable to the case and plug it into the mains but leave all the power switches off.

5 Now clip your anti-static strap to a bare-metal part of the case. Congratulations, you've now put the first two parts of your system together and will protect all the others from the evil of static.

Important

The static straps are designed to pop off so that when you walk away from the PC you don't drag the case behind you. However, get used to unclipping it before you move away to prevent the wire pinging around the case or sending bits and pieces flying across your desk.

With your body safely protected against static build up, you can now unpack the main components of your system: the motherboard, processor, cooling and memory. They will all be wrapped in anti-static bags and lots of packing to prevent damage in transit. Keep them in their bags until you are at the point of actually putting them into the PC. To remove any piece of hardware you should open the box or bag and grasp the hardware around the edges with thumb and fore finger, or with both hands in the case of the motherboard. Try not to touch any of the circuitry or parts.

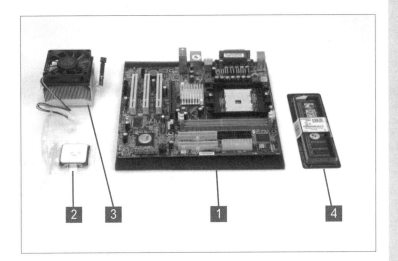

1. Motherboard: Ensure the board is sitting neatly on the foam mat to cushion the underside while you install the parts.

2. Processor: Keep this in its immediate packaging until you are ready to install it.

3. Cooler: Keep the bottom plastic cover on the cooler to protect the thermal paste.

4. Memory: Leave this in its bag or plastic case until you come to install it.

3

Jargon buster

Thermal Paste – this is a chemical compound, usually including silicon, silver or another metal that has good thermal properties, used to lift heat from the processor and pass it up to the cooling block and fan. It fills in the small dents and imperfections between the metals to aid conductivity.

Installing the processor

Most motherboards come on a foam sheet and you should leave yours lying on this to prevent damage to the underside as you push down on the top when installing the parts. The first thing to do is add the most valuable piece of equipment, the processor. Pick it up, holding it between thumb and forefinger around the plastic edge; you can see two very different sides. The actual chip lies under the metal shield you can see on the upper surface. On the underside you will see the pins or contacts that connect the hundreds of different data lines to the rest of the system. On one corner of the plastic will be an arrow that indicates how the chip should fit into the motherboard slot.

With AMD and older Intel processors, the pins are on the underside of the chip. With newer Intel designs, the pins are on the board while the contact points are on the chip. With both systems you need to lift the arm on the side of the processor socket to unlock it. On new Intel systems there is an extra lid to be lifted. In most instances, there is some protective plastic that will need to be removed from the motherboard socket.

You can then insert the processor by lining up the arrow on the chip with the one on the motherboard. These arrows indicate the first pin of the chip. The whole chip package is designed so that it cannot be installed incorrectly. If the chip doesn't drop neatly into the socket then pick it up and try again. Once the chip drops in neatly you can close the lid and/or arm to relock the system and secure the chip on the motherboard.

See also

Installing an AMD processor, and Installing an Intel processor take you through this procedure step-by-step.

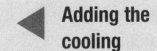

One of the scariest parts of building a PC comes next. The processor generates a lot of heat and, on older systems, could literally melt without a cooling system. Today's chips, however, should automatically shut down before heat damage can occur. A modern PC cooling system consists of a layer of thermal paste that sits between the processor and the heatsink (an array of aluminium fins that help take heat off the processor and dissipate it). Finally, there's a fan on top of the heatsink to keep air circulating, moving the warm air away from the processor block.

If you bought a consumer processor then it will have come with a cooling system supplied. If you purchased an OEM model then you will have chosen your own cooling system. The latter could have been a basic stock model or there are many exotic and advanced systems that can keep temperatures lower and extend the life of your system. Some cooling systems have larger than average fans that run slower and more quietly to reduce noise. At the very exotic end of the range, there are water-cooling systems that will run silently.

Any cooler that came with your chip should come out of the packaging with a plastic tray at the bottom. Only remove this cover when you're actually ready to install the cooler. When the CPU is correctly in place and you're feeling confident, lift off the cover and you'll see the paste that will sit on top of the processor shield, providing a solid bond between chip and cooler. Align the cooler with the motherboard mounting. Depending on the motherboard make and

processor type, these can be fitted in several ways: AMD coolers have arms that move and lock down onto mounts on the motherboard; Intel coolers have pins that are pushed into place.

Whatever the type, you need to use a degree of force to lock them into place. Applying a lot of pressure on something so fragile looking may seem counter-intuitive but it has to be done to get a good connection between cooler and processor. With AMD chips, you need to pull one of the arms down and get the clips over the holders at the bottom. It's the second arm that requires a lot of force. Some AMD coolers have a hinged arm that helps control the amount of force properly and will make the task a little easier. Intel users will see four pins or legs on the corners that need to be pushed vertically down into place. Again major force is required to get them to lock into place. Just remain calm and keep pushing until they lock.

After you've got over the exertion of locking the cooler into place don't forget that you need to connect its power lead. This lead has a two- or four-pin connection and there will be a matching connector on the board right next to the cooler site. Make sure the connection is made firmly and you will now have finished the most stressful part of building a PC.

See also

Instructions on pages 46 and 53 take you through this procedure step-by-step.

3

Installing an AMD processor

The photos in this section show how to install the processor on an AMD-based system. If you've gone the Intel route then skip forward a few pages to page 49 to find your processor and the method for installing it on the Intel-style motherboard.

1 Take a look on the board at the square white socket for the processor. You'll see a metal arm on one side. It is held in place by a small tab. Apply a small amount of pressure to free the arm and lift it up.

2 This exposes the contacts in the socket so you can insert the processor. When the arm is locked back down it will hold the processor firmly in place.

3 Now pick up your processor holding it firmly with your fingers around the edge. In one corner of the processor there's a small golden triangle.

4 A mark on the corner of the socket diagonally opposite to where the metal bar pivots matches the triangle on the processor. Align these two markings such that they will be one above the other when the processor is lowered onto the socket.

5 With the processor held horizontally over the socket on the motherboard, lower it gently into place. If inserted correctly the pins will vanish into their sockets and you'll see only the plastic edge of the chip. If this doesn't happen, lift it up and try again, ensuring the triangles match.

6 Once the processor is fitted snugly into the socket, lower the metal bar ensuring that it clips back into place. This will lock the processor firmly into place and ensure a good contact for data to flow into the chip when the system is running.

3

Jargon buster

Pins – each pin on a processor is the physical connection to a data wire on the motherboard that links the processor to the other parts of the system.

Installing an AMD processor (cont.)

7 Well done, that's the finesse part of this task completed. The end result should look just like this photo.

8 Note the black plastic fort-shaped edging surrounding the processor. This is the fitting to hold the cooler.

9 Remove the packaging from your cooler and take off the plastic cover at the bottom that protects the thermal paste. Check that the paste is a clean square with no sign of thin streaks or blobs.

Installing an AMD processor (cont.)

10 Align it to the motherboard so that the metal clips on the side will slot onto the black plastic notches on the cooler fitting. Hold the cooler horizontally over the newly-fitted processor and lower it into place. It should fit snugly and squarely over the processor. Now move one of the metal clips down and clip it over the plastic hook, making sure that it goes all the way over the plastic and is securely restrained.

11 On older systems you had to push with reckless force to clip the second clip over the plastic notch, but modern AMD coolers come with a useful lever to take some of the strain. So, push the clip into place (it still takes a little force) and then push the lever all the way down.

Installing an AMD processor (cont.)

12 If all's gone well the cooler should be mounted on the processor as solidly as a rock. This happy relationship will keep heat moving away from the processor thereby allowing it to run without cooking itself.

13 The last act in this part of the installation is to connect the power lead for the cooler. Somewhere in the vicinity will be a small white power connector with three prongs that will match the wire coming out of the cooler. It will only fit one way round so ensure you line it up properly and push it firmly into place.

Jargon buster

Heatsink – this specially designed metal construction is used to absorb heat from the processor. The heat is then dispersed by the fan to prevent the chip from overheating. A modern processor can run happily at up to 50–60°C; any higher and you might want better cooling or there may be a problem.

The photos in this section show how to install the processor on an Intel-based system. It is done roughly in the same sequence as its AMD counterpart but there are several structural differences in how everything connects.

For your information

If you want to find out more about your processor then you can find out the details and how it compares to other Intel models at the web page:
http://indigo.intel.com/compare_cpu/default.aspx?familyID=1

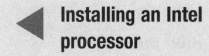

Installing an Intel processor

1 Intel processor sockets are shiny metal affairs that come with several moving parts. Your first task is to unclip the metal arm and lift it to open up the whole socket.

2 There is usually a plastic warning tag inside the socket. This can be removed to expose the pins that will connect the processor to the motherboard.

3

Installing an Intel processor (cont.)

3. Now lift up the metal shield so that the socket is ready to take the processor. At this point check for the triangle that points to the first pin; there will be a reciprocal triangle on the processor.

4. Unpack your Intel processor and hold it firmly around the edges.

5. You'll need to remove the plastic cover from the underside of the processor to install it. Find the triangle on one of the corners and rotate the chip so that it's the right orientation to fit over the triangle on the socket.

Installing an Intel processor (cont.)

6 Now hold the chip flat over the socket, ensuring that the two triangles are aligned correctly. Lower it gently into place until it fits neatly into the socket.

7 The result should look something like this. If the processor doesn't look as if it's sitting flat or squarely, lift it out and try again, ensuring the triangles are aligned correctly.

3

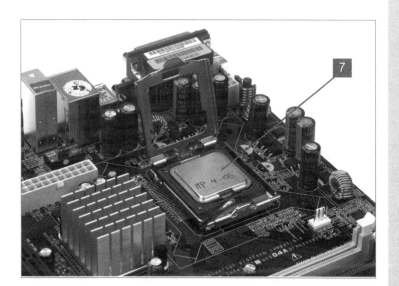

Installing an Intel processor (cont.)

8 Now lower the shield down over the processor to secure it. Pull down on the lever to lock everything into place. Ensure that it clips in to remain locked in the down position.

9 That's your processor fitted all nice and neatly. If you compare the Intel board to an AMD model you'll notice there's no cooler housing. Instead there are four holes into which four prongs on the base of the cooler can clip.

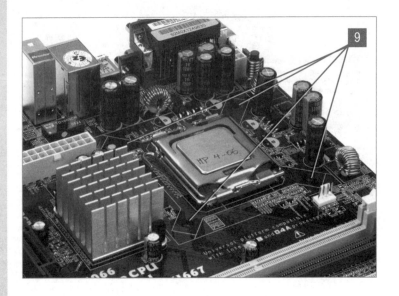

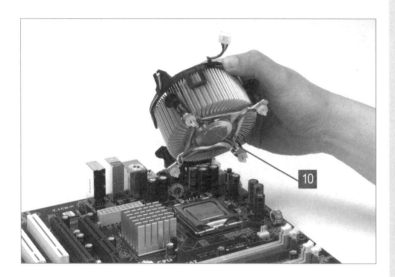

10 Get the cooler out of its packaging and check that there's a neat square of thermal paste at the bottom. Remove any extra packaging and get ready to place its paste square on top of the processor.

11 Make sure there's enough lead on the cooler power cable to fit into its socket and then lower the cooler over the processor so that the four pins, one on each corner, sit over the holes in the motherboard.

12 You'll need to press down quite firmly to get them to clip in and once done there should be a very firm connection between processor and cooler.

3

Installing an Intel processor (cont.)

13 Now clip the cooler power lead into its power connector that will be nearby. It will only fit one way round so ensure you line it up properly and push it firmly into place.

Installing your memory

4

Introduction

Memory can be added to an installed motherboard but you usually have to fight your way past a jungle of wires and it can often be fiddly work. So we might as well make use of all this open space while it's available. Making sure you've still got your anti-static strip on, take a look at the motherboard and examine the memory sockets. At each end there's a plastic hook that will match the notches on your memory sticks. You'll also see there's a small gap on the connector block that's slightly off-centre and a corresponding notch in the bottom of the memory stick. This is to ensure you fit the memory the correct way.

Some motherboards have two, three or even four slots for memory. These should be labelled bank one, two, three and four and are often colour coded. The colour coding will help if you are installing a matched pair of memory sticks. Many recent motherboards allow for dual channel memory access, meaning that the PC can talk to two banks of memory at the same time. If your board has two yellow memory slots and one orange one, then install your dual-channel RAM in the two yellow ones for faster-performing memory. If you are mixing old and new memory then, assuming it's compatible in the first place, put the fastest RAM in the first slot and the older ram in the highest numbered slot.

There are three main types of RAM used in PCs today. DDR memory is the most common; DDR-II is slowly becoming a common type; and on some, usually high-end boards, RD-RAM is used. Check that you get the right type of memory for your motherboard and, if the board takes multiple memory types, ensure they go in the right banks.

What you'll do

Add memory to the motherboard

Install the motherboard

Connect your system

Install your graphics card

Jargon buster

Dual-channel memory – memory makers have invented many tricks to make memory access faster. Dual channel is the latest of these. It allows the processor to talk to both banks of memory at the same time. To achieve this trick, the two sticks of memory have to be exactly the same type, called a matched pair, because the timing of communication between them and the processor is critical.

Adding memory to the motherboard

After the complexities of the processor and cooler, adding memory is quite straightforward. All you need to do is open up the clips on the side of the motherboard's RAM slot and press the memory sticks into place.

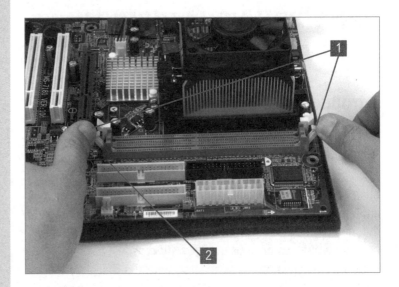

1 Push the clips back on the edge of the bank where you want to install your stick of RAM.

2 There is usually a bank number on one side; fill bank one first.

Important

When you come to install your memory, hold it by the edges with two hands and line it up the correct way over the memory slot. Then, place it vertically into the slot and push down with both thumbs equally spaced across the top of the stick. You'll hear a click and see the hooks move in to secure the memory in place. Historically these hooks aren't the most secure things so, if they don't move completely into the hole on the memory stick, push them gently into place. That's that job done unless you have multiple sticks of memory in which case you just repeat the process.

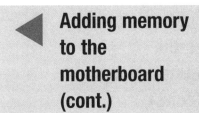
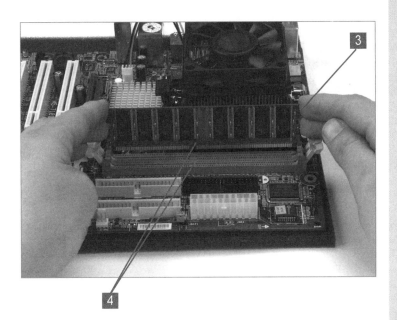

3 Take your RAM out of its static bag holding it by the edges.

4 Hold it over the bank and check that the memory's notch and the small gap in the contact strip match up.

4

Adding memory to the motherboard (cont.)

5 Push the RAM firmly down into the bank and the clips should pop up to hold it in place.

6 Sometimes they don't pop up fully, however, and you might need to nudge the clips in to ensure the memory is firmly seated.

You've loaded your naked motherboard with all the expensive parts, so let's get on with installing it into the case. Ensure that your wrist strap is on before you touch anything, especially if you've been away for a well-earned cup of tea after putting all the components together so far.

Your first task will be to switch the backplate on the case for the one that comes with your motherboard. Then you'll have to prepare the case by screwing in a number of stand-offs that stop the motherboard coming in contact with the side of the case and causing a short circuit. Next we get to install the motherboard, firmly screwing it into place and making sure it fits to the back of the case where all the connectors will go.

 ## Installing the motherboard

---

1 On the back of the case there will be an original backplate, a rectangular piece of metal with punched, shaped holes for all the connectors (such as the monitor cable and audio wires) to go through. Unless you're very lucky, it will most likely not look the same as the one your motherboard came with.

4

Overview

2 Remove this original backplate. First, just try pushing it from the inside to see if it pops out. If that doesn't work and it's just held in place by metal links, then pushing it backwards and forwards until the links open enough should do the job. If the case maker was thoughtful enough to attach it with screws, just unscrew it.

Lying your case down with the open side facing up, you'll see that there are screw holes sticking up in lines, some of these, but probably not all, will match the holes you can see in your motherboard. There are several sizes of board so don't expect all the holes to be used. With the motherboard came a package of screws and bolts. Inside it will be a number of brass or plastic spacers, also called stand offs. You have to put these between the board and the case screw holes to insulate it.

Some boards come with a smart tray feature that will slide out and make installation easier as you can do it outside the confines of the case. In either case the process is largely similar. Hold the motherboard over your case and note where the holes match. Screw a spacer into each hole that matches the holes in your board. Not all designs are the same so you might not need to fill every hole.

You can now place your board into the case. Carefully fit it so that the screw holes line up and your bank of connectors fits correctly with the metal sheet you fitted earlier. These connectors often require a bit of jiggling and pushing on the metal panel to pop them all through, just take it easy and be patient. Make sure there's a spacer for each hole on your motherboard. Ensure you haven't missed one. Then start tightening a screw into each hole in a logical fashion so you don't miss one. This process requires some finesse and care.

Do not over-tighten these screws as you could crack the motherboard thereby possibly destroying it in one false move. Be very careful too with your screwdriver as one slip there could also spell the end of your system. Finally, if you happen to drop a screw on the board then you'll need to retrieve it with a pair of plastic pliers or other non-conductive implement to prevent possible damage. Hopefully you'll make it through this step unscathed and will have a board sitting neatly in its case. The following instructions provide more detail about each step of this process.

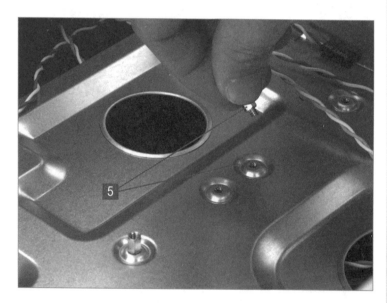

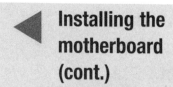

Installing the motherboard (cont.)

Step-by-step

3 Put your plate into position from the inside of the case, checking that it is the right way up. Any small metal clips or springs should be facing inside the case. Push the plate firmly into place.

4 In most circumstances the two topmost holes will be round ones and these should go nearest the power supply.

5 Work out which of the holes on the inside of the case will need the brass/plastic screws to fit the motherboard. Do this by holding the board over the case and visually checking where the screw holes are. Then get the right number of spacer screws and put them into place.

4

Installing the motherboard (cont.)

▶

6. Now lower the motherboard into position, holding it carefully around the edges. Aim to place it in as closely as possible so that the holes and screws are lined up and you won't have to nudge it unnecessarily.

7. A little gentle pushing may be required to line up all the holes properly and to get the connectors to pop through the plate. Push the board gently around from the edge in small movements to get it right.

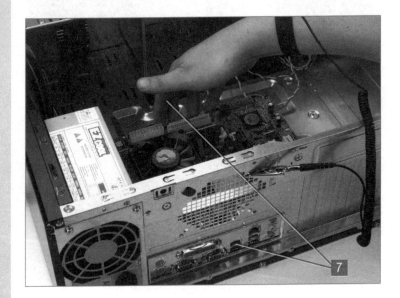

8 Now screw the motherboard into place. There is only one type of screw from the several types that come with the board that will fit into the brass/plastic connectors. Try them out on a spare connector before fitting them to the case. Remember: do not over-tighten any of the screws, just work until they are solidly in place.

4

Important

You need to make sure your motherboard can't touch the bare metal of the case. The spacers prevent this. If a contact is made when the system is on then there could be a short circuit.

Connecting your system

With the board in place, the time has now come to wire up all the various parts of your board and case together. The first item to link up will be the main power supply to the motherboard. There are two distinct power blocks coming from the power supply. One is small and square, the second is larger and rectangular. These need to be plugged into the board, generally, somewhere near the memory banks. There's only one place each on the board that these blocks will connect to and they should be obvious; one socket is square, the other rectangular. Both plugs have a hooked tab on one side and need to be oriented such that each hook clips over a corresponding ridge on one side of its socket.

For your information

Case wiring – when first inspecting the case you should have seen a clutch of thin wires ending in black connectors. These link the power button, case lights and any front panel USB and audio connectors to the motherboard. Expensive modern cases can have lots of extra features like card readers, temperature sensors and other gizmos that may need also wiring up.

Timesaver tip

Before you install the power supply into the computer it is always worth testing that the unit works by plugging it in and flicking on the power switch briefly to ensure that the fan spins up and any lights work. You'll only be disappointed if you screw it into place without checking only to find later on that nothing works.

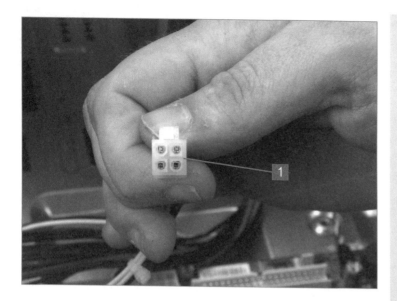

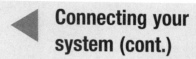

Connecting your system (cont.)

Step-by-step

1 From the loom of wires coming out of the power supply are a host of power connectors. Find the small white square block with a tab on one side.

2 Somewhere on the motherboard there will be a square socket mounting similar in size to the wired block. Insert the plug into the socket such that its tab is oriented to clip over the ridge on the socket.

4

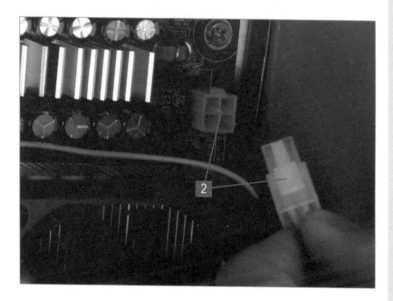

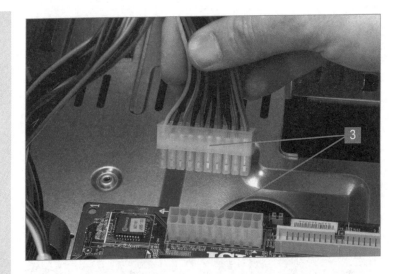

Overview

 Now connect the larger rectangular block; again there is a clip on one side that dictates the only way it will fit to the connector on the board. This block is usually found among the drive connectors and is easily located.

The next set of wires we'll connect come from the case itself. There are lots of little clusters of black connectors with writing on them. These belong to the front control panel, the power button and any other features your case might have. You'll need to attach the power and light connectors, otherwise you won't be able to turn the computer on. The USB and audio connectors are optional to fix but it makes sense to do so, rather than reaching behind the PC every time you want to plug in your headphones or connect a digital camera. These little wires all fit somewhere on the motherboard, usually around the edges but it'll take a check of the manual to figure out exactly where. Generally, although it can vary, the connectors can be found on the bottom edge of the motherboard. They're the small rectangular clusters of pins pointing up from the board. By the pins, printed on the board, will be brief descriptions, but with very limited space you're better checking in the manual.

You may also find that what's written on the end of a lead isn't the same as what you'll see in the manual. If you're lucky the case documentation (it may just be a thin sheet of paper the size of a post-it note) will have a translation that should resemble what is listed in the motherboard manual. The manual schematic will show where to install each connector. Take this process gently as you don't want to bend or break the pins. Start with the power and light buttons, as they're essential and the easiest to match. Any USB connectors should come next and, finally, you're left with the jungle of audio wires. These vary in design; for example, the internal speaker may look like a regular little speaker, bolted to the side of the case or it may be a tiny black cylinder that comes loose with the motherboard. The headphone and microphone leads consist of five wires each and their connectors will most likely have jumpers over them, this is to disable them as the rear ones will already be 'live' through the motherboard. You'll need to remove the jumpers if you want to add these connections to the front panel. The following instructions provide more detail about each step of this process.

Step-by-step

4 Pick up the bundle of wires that run to the front of the case.

5 The text on these wires is basically gibberish so check in the motherboard manual to see where each one connects.

6 It will point out exactly which connector fits in what pin in each of the blocks.

4

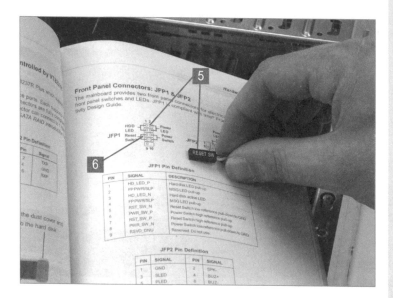

For your information

If you can't work out where the various leads connect on the motherboard then investigate both the motherboard manual and any documentation that came with the case for clarification.

Connecting your system (cont.)

7 When you've found out where the pins go, push them into place one by one. If you're dexterous enough you might manage to do two at a time, which makes things a little easier.

8 The remaining wires are for audio and USB connectors. Your case might not have them depending on its design. Again you'll need to check against the manual as to where they are fitted. As there are already audio connectors on the back panel, you may find small jumper blocks in place where you'll want to plug them in; just remove them to keep them safe.

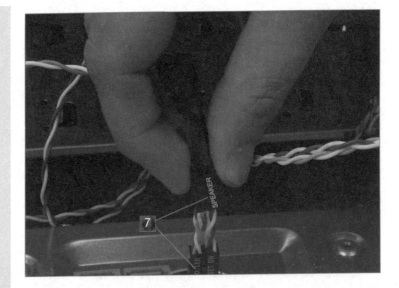

With the case now wired in and power supplied to the motherboard, the last act is to connect your spanking new graphics card. The graphics card on your system does all the donkey work of converting data into pictures and sending them down the cable to your monitor. If your motherboard has video built in then you can use it directly without a video card but almost all PC users get a decent video card for high performance graphics.

Installing your graphics card

1 Look at the back of the case and you'll see the long slots on the motherboard where the peripherals connect. One will look different to the others, often a different colour; it will be your AGP or PCI bus slot. At the end of it will be the end plate on the case where the video lead will plug in. Your first step will be to undo the retaining screw and lift out the plate, keeping the screw safe. Some cheaper motherboards do away with the screws and just have sheets of thin metal that you waggle to get loose and remove.

2 Make sure the little catch at the end of the bus is in the open position.

3 Then remove your graphics card from its box and static bag and, holding it by the edges, lower it into place. You should slot its edge into its bus and push down from above but a little wiggling may help slot it in.

4 Make sure the end plate of the card is flush against the case.

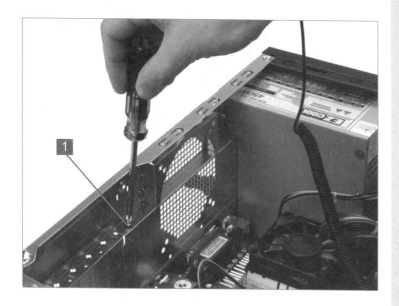

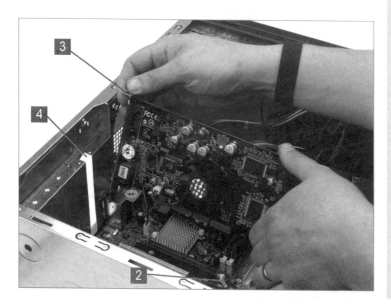

4

Installing your graphics card (cont.)

5. Ensure the catch has closed after the card is fitted to make sure it is locked in place. Historically, graphics cards could pop out while running, causing all manner of panic and damage, so these catches are a welcome addition to PC design.

6. Now lock the graphics card firmly into place using the original screw. Use a screw from the motherboard box if your case didn't use screws to hold the plates in place. If there's resistance to lining the plate up here check that the bottom of the plate has fitted between the motherboard and the side of the case.

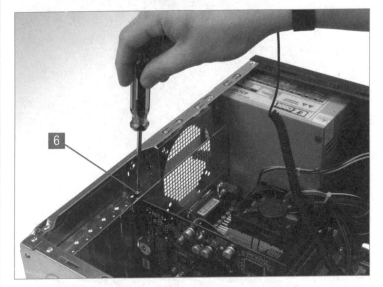

Timesaver tip

More-powerful modern graphics cards require a power connector identical to the one that attaches to your hard disk or DVD drive. The card will have come supplied with a junction cable in case you don't have any spare connectors once all your drives are connected. If you do have a spare connector (which the majority of users will have these days) just plug it in directly.

Connecting your storage

5

Introduction

Your computer is almost complete but you still need to add the drives to allow for storage. A minor choice here is where to put things. Most case designs incorporate many drive bays. If the system is to stand on the floor, then the DVD drive should be situated at the top of the tower, but if it's going on a desk then you might want the DVD drive in the lowest position. The floppy drive generally peeks out somewhere in the middle of the case and the hard drive remains hidden inside. Installing and wiring them up should pose little challenge after the previous tasks; all of them are fixed to the housing at the front of the case by screws and, with up to eight screws per drive. There's a lot of manual labour involved.

Before connecting your storage you will probably need to remove a metal plate or two from the inside front of the case. This is done by rocking the plate backwards and forwards, often with some vigour, until it comes out. Then you'll need to pop out the plastic face plates for the optical and floppy drives from the front of the case. These are usually held in by plastic clips that you can move with fingers and thumbs or the gentle application of a screwdriver.

To complete this job properly, you'll need to have both sides of the case removed in order to fix the screws into opposite sides of each drive. Some luxury cases have cunning mechanisms for doing away with screws altogether but for the majority of us its time for a marathon effort with the trusty Philips. It's best to put all the drives in first before attempting to wire them up. Once they're all firmly bolted in place, it's time to plug them in.

What you'll do

Install your DVD drive

Connect a SATA drive

Connect an IDE drive

Finish off your PC build

Installing your DVD drive

The essential hard drive and the latest DVD burner are all that's left between us and a complete computer; with a humble floppy drive making an invaluable addition if you want to complete the family. Taking a little care, let's get on with finishing your machine.

1 Many cases have metal plates obstructing the DVD drive bays for no apparent reason. This part of the task is a good candidate for picking up a bleeding digit so don't get too carried away trying to tear the plate out.

2 This is the hunk of metal you've just removed. It's now completely useless and probably bent out of shape so you can consign it to the dustbin and congratulate yourself if you've managed to get away without a scratch or cut.

3 Now remove the equivalent
front cover plate. These usually
have two catches that you just
need to tweak from the inside
of the case to pop the whole
thing out.

4 Now unpack your DVD drive
and slide it neatly into place.
You'll want the front face of
the drive flat with the edges of
the case.

5 Screw holes in the sides of
the drive should finish up in
line with holes in the drive bay.

5

Installing your
DVD drive (cont.)

6 Now fix the drive into place with screws from the motherboard package (use the most numerous type of screw). To be thorough, you should use four screws on each side, but if you're in a hurry you can put two per side on opposite corners and it's unlikely any harm will be done.

7 Take the same approach for the floppy disk drive, if you're adding one to your system, and fix it in place. If you don't want a plain drive you can get more impressive units with memory-card readers built in to make them slightly more useful.

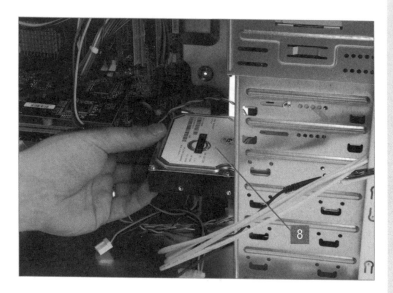

8 The hard disk drive is slotted into place from the inside. You'll find narrow rails inside the drive bay that it will rest on. Line up the screw holes and then fix it firmly into place. That's the bulky work done, now its time to connect up the drives.

5

Connecting a SATA drive

As discussed in the buying section, SATA is the latest standard connection for hard drives and helps them run a little faster than they do with the IDE predecessor. The most practical benefit gained with SATA, though, is that its leads are thinner and easier to manipulate in the confines of a case. At both ends these cables have neat fittings that ensure you can only plug them in the right way round. One very good reason to get a SATA drive is that this page covers the entire process.

1. Find a SATA port on the motherboard. There are often two so you can have multiple drives on the one system. Plug one end of the cable into this.

2. Connect the cable to the drive, check the alignment of the cable and push until you feel it slot into place.

3. Using a SATA power adapter to plug in the standard large power connectors, connect this to the lead coming from the PSU.

4. Then plug it into the disk drive.

For your information

If you have a modern power supply it may already have SATA power cables coming out of it thereby eliminating one lead.

There are two leads for each drive, a power cable from the PSU and a data cable that will plug into the motherboard. Drive cables, particular IDE types, the wide flat ones, come pre-folded, maybe with a band or tape around them. If possible its nice to keep them that way so try to wire up the cables using the shortest route to prevent cables clogging up the inside of the case. Sometimes though it just doesn't work out that way so don't worry too much if you end up with a tangle of wires inside.

Take a look at your motherboard near the drive bays. There should be three obvious data connectors and matching cables in the motherboard box. The narrower connector and lead is for the floppy drive while two wider examples are for your hard disk and DVD drive. Modern computers have two channels, represented by the two connectors on the motherboard. A little maths will show that you can have up to four hard or optical drives connected at once. Plug an IDE cable, which should have come supplied with your motherboard, into the number one IDE connector. There will be two plugs on each cable, the one at the far end of the cable is the primary and one in the middle is the secondary. The primary connector should always go to the fastest drive, which in a race between hard disk and optical drive will always be won by the hard drive. If you only have one hard and one optical drive then the ideal way to connect them is to make the hard disk the primary drive and the optical drive secondary. This means you only need the one cable.

Connecting an IDE drive

For your information

Setting the jumpers – this issue is confused slightly by a jumper that you'll find on both the hard and DVD drives. You can set each drive to one of three settings, master, slave and cable select. As your hard drive will be the primary, that wants to be called master; the optical should be the slave. Just remember that these jumpers will need setting again if you decide to add more drives at a later date. With all that done, your IDE drives should now be ready to go and your computer is all but built.

5

Connecting an
IDE drive (cont.)

1. You should already have found the drive connectors on the motherboard.

2. Take one of the drive cables and connect it to the primary channel connector (see 1). Push it firmly into place, noting the notch that will only allow it to fit one way.

3. Now connect the connector in the middle of the cable to the DVD drive, assuming it'll reach, and the end connector to the hard drive. Again there's a notch to ensure these fit the right way around.

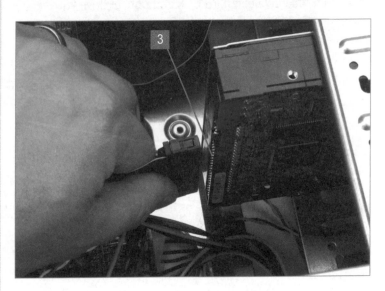

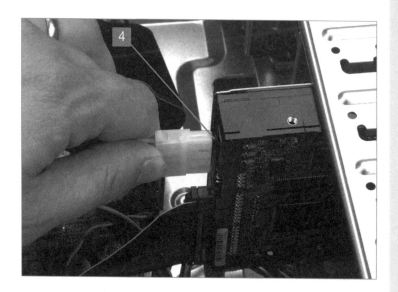

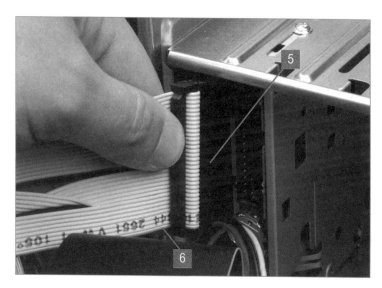

4 The power connectors for the hard and DVD drives come from the power supply. They have angled corners on one side so these too will only connect in one orientation, no matter how hard you try. Give these a very firm push to ensure they're plugged in tightly.

5 The floppy drive has narrower data and power cables. The power cable has a different shaped connector that may take a couple of goes to attach correctly. The key is the thin notch on the all-plastic side.

6 The data cable has a twisted part in it (this is a legacy of machines having more than one floppy drive) and a red edge which should connect to pin number one of the floppy.

5

7 Connect the drive cable to the thinner of the motherboard connectors and that's the last major step in building your PC. At this point take a good look at all the connections and make sure everything is firmly installed.

Take a step back and admire your handiwork, the result should be many hundreds of pounds of expensive kit neatly installed with no panic or damage. The last steps in finishing your PC off are the simple, mundane things. Many cases come with the feet detached so you can plug these into the bottom of the case. You can then turn the case upright and connect your peripherals and monitor before giving the system a test run.

At this point you might want to leave the case open in case there is a startup problem with the system or, if confident, you can seal the system up and get ready to let it run.

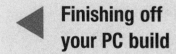

Finishing off your PC build

5

Connecting your storage 81

Finishing off your PC build (cont.)

1 The rubber or plastic feet will help prevent some vibration and protect your desktop from possible scratches so try not to forget to put them on the bottom of the case.

2 Most new mice and keyboards have rectangular USB connectors, but if you want to preserve your USB ports for more important items you can still get leads with the old style round PS-2 connectors which are still part of all PCs.

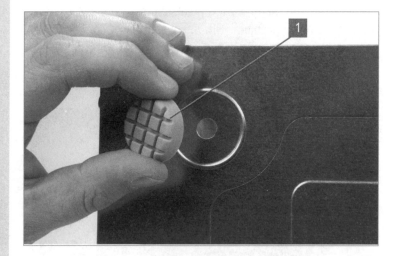

Installing Windows on a new PC

Introduction

Your new PC is sitting there waiting to be used. Until an operating system is installed, however, there is nothing you can do other than admire it or use the case as a large paperweight. Windows is used on about 98% of all PCs around the world so we expect you'll be doing the same. If you want to install another operating system such as Linux then the instructions are broadly similar but each version of Linux has its own way of doing things.

Windows XP is currently the standard version of Windows but, if you're feeling brave, then a beta version of Windows Vista can be downloaded so you get to try out the next generation of Windows early. It is also likely that a version of the Mac operating system called OS/X will be released for PC systems, but this remains to be seen.

For your information

Windows Vista should be available for us to buy in the shops in early 2007. If you want to try it out early then a beta version can be ordered on DVD or your can download the 3 GB file from www.microsoft.com/windowsvista/getready/default.mspx. You need to register for the service and we should point out that being a beta, a lot of its technology is still work in progress, so this is not recommended to be used on your main PC, but it's a good way to get a glimpse of the future early.

What you'll do

Format your hard drive

Install Windows files

Enter important details

Jargon buster

Linux – an operating system that is very different to Windows, Linux is based around industrial strength code that is less likely to crash but more complicated to manage. Modern Linux has a similar graphical interface to Windows but underneath is still a command-based language with many commands and parameters that have to be learned.

Formatting your hard drive ▶

1 At first you'll just see a black screen for a minute while the installer program checks out your computer.

2 Then you'll see a blue screen with some text while it loads some basic driver files that can run on any hardware. You can see them loading in the bottom left-hand corner.

Most of us have blissfully seen our previous shiny new PCs arrive with Windows XP happily installed and running. This isn't an option for anyone building their own system so we'll cover the process in detail to make sure your computer is running at maximum efficiency. To install Windows XP from scratch takes around 45 minutes, with an additional hour or so for the operating system to get all the drivers and hardware correctly functioning.

Most of the process is spent just watching the screen and pressing Enter occasionally, but there are a few options you can change and, once Windows is actually installed, there's a lot more fine-tuning that can be done.

When you switch on your computer, not much will happen past the POST test because no operating system has been installed. To install Windows you need to put your XP CD in the drive and restart the machine. Most systems will boot from the CD automatically and you'll be launched into the Windows XP setup program.

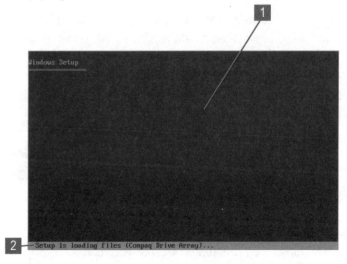

84

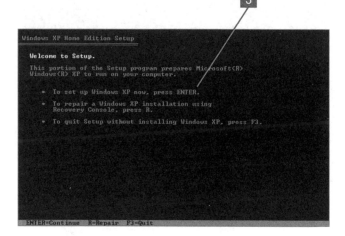

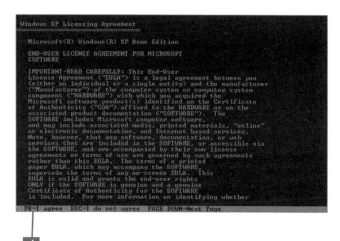

Formatting your hard drive (cont.)

3 Your Windows XP disk is a versatile asset that can be used to fix a broken installation or reinstall over a dead one. However, as we're starting from scratch, just press Enter to start the installation process.

4 Before you can install Windows you'll need to accept the license agreement. Just press F8 to agree to the license. We don't know a single human being who has read the whole thing but, basically, you agree not to pirate or alter the code inside Windows.

For your information

The recovery console is a very technical process. If ever you can't boot into Windows, however, then using the disk provides a useful recovery point.

Jargon buster

POST – Power On Self Test is a series of checks the computer carries out on itself to ensure all is well with the main hardware components.

6

Formatting your hard drive (cont.)

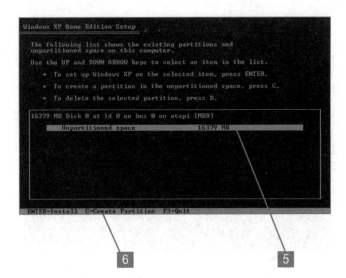

5 Choose where you want the operating system installed. In almost all cases this will be on your 'C:' drive, another name for the primary hard disk drive. Press Enter to install Windows to the chosen drive. In reality you'll rarely have an option unless you've added a range of partitions or have multiple hard disks in your machine.

6 Press C if you want to split your hard disk into different chunks. Unless you have a good reason to do so we don't recommend this.

For your information

A hard disk drive starts out as a big empty void, ready to be tuned for use in many types of system. They can also be broken up into separate sections to make multiple virtual drives. In years past, this was useful because Windows could only see drives up to a certain size. Also, different users could have their own chunk of space. But all of this is largely irrelevant in the current Windows age. Today almost all users are happy just to have one big chunk of disk space. To install Windows you need to partition and format the drive. In practice this is a simple process but one fraught with acronyms and strange concepts.

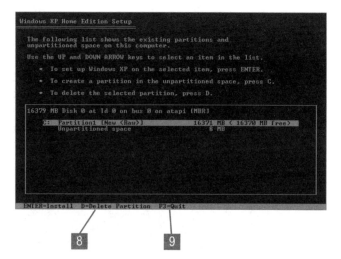

7 Press Enter again to create a partition of the maximum available size. Again this is the recommended step. If you do want multiple partitions then make the primary partition 50% of the available space and create a secondary partition of the same size; you can vary these as required. Sometimes there is a little space left in the unpartitioned space field. This is normal and can be ignored.

8 Now that we have a partitioned drive, you need to format it. This is a process that allows Windows to be able to write data to it. Formatting a drive brings us our first major choice: between two types of formatting known as NTFS and FAT. If you're not happy with what you've done at this point then you can press D to delete the partition.

9 If you're having concerns about the process then you can press F3 to abandon installing Windows for now.

Jargon buster

NTFS – the New Technology File System is actually decades old and is a better organised version of the FAT file system that Windows 98 and its predecessors used to employ.

FAT – File Allocation Table refers to the old way Windows stored details about files and folders. Windows 95 used a 16-bit version called FAT-16 while 98 started using FAT-32 which doubled the amount of hard drive space that Windows could read.

6

Formatting your hard drive (cont.)

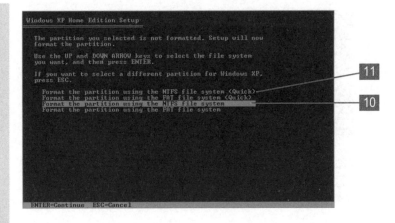

10 Windows XP replaced the old FAT file system with NTFS. Unless you have a pressing reason for backwards compatibility with some Windows 98-only programs then choose NTFS. The full version of the format is more thorough and it is worth taking the time to do, particularly if you're using an old drive. A full format will ensure any errors on the hard disk are spotted and marked so they won't be used by Windows

11 A quick format should also be fine.

12 Whatever option you've chosen for formatting, sit back for a while as the drive is arranged for use. This makes it readable to the operating system.

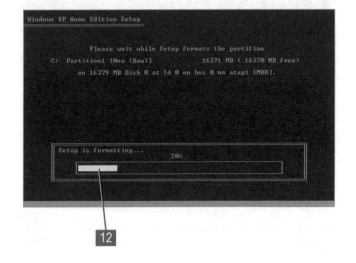

Have a good magazine and a cup of tea on standby for this part of the process as most of it is about watching progress bars roll slowly along. The bulk of this time is spent with files being copied from archives on the CD and then extracted to their correct folders on the hard disk. You have some input on this process by choosing a range of details to enter, including your location, so elements like time zones, keyboard layout and other information can be accurately set.

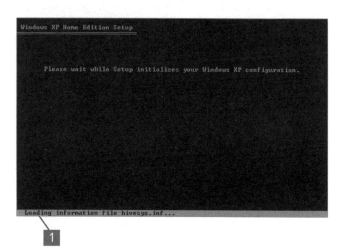

Installing Windows files

1 Once formatting is complete, Windows XP will load a host of files from the CD onto the hard disk so that installation can begin. You can see these listed in the lower right-hand corner and the task will take a few minutes.

2 Once the previous step is complete, Windows XP will need to restart the computer so that it can begin working from the hard drive. Leave your CD in that drive and press Enter if you want to speed the timer bar along.

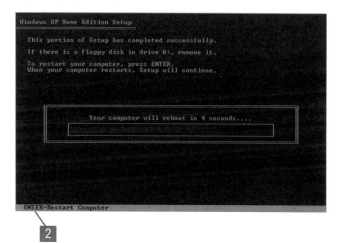

6

Installing Windows files (cont.)

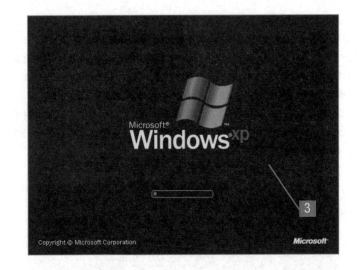

3 When Windows starts loading you'll see this screen; just wait until the main installer screen pops up.

4 Next you'll see this screen that has a list of tasks on the left-hand side of the screen.

5 There's also a description of features in XP on the right but you should be familiar with most of them already.

6 Towards the bottom left is an approximation of time remaining to complete the installation. A lot of the process is automatic but you need to stick around to choose some of your basic settings.

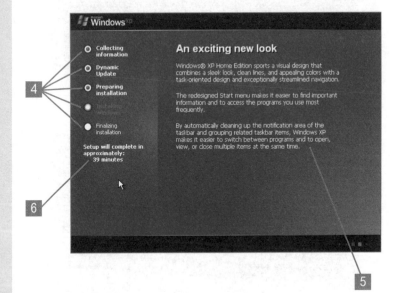

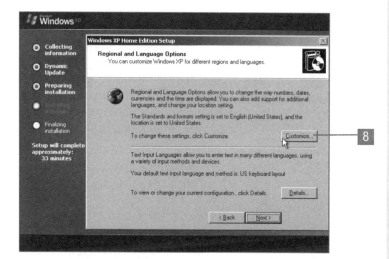

Installing Windows files (cont.)

7 As the various processes run you'll see this progress bar with an explanation of what's currently going on.

8 After some time copying the required files over, you can start configuring XP to your needs. The first thing to do is tell the computer where you are and what language you'll be using. By default Windows will use US English which has several significant differences to ours, so let's set our machine up for British English using the Customize button to start.

6

Installing Windows files (cont.)

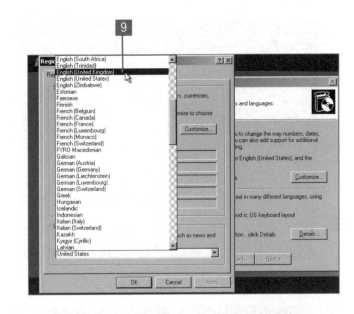

9   Scroll down the list and set your language to English (United Kingdom). You can have multiple language support in Windows but setting UK English as the primary language is essential for using the '£' and other local symbols.

10 Ensure your default settings are for English (United Kingdom) for all of the settings.

11 Most important is the keyboard, as some symbols are located in different places on other nation's key layouts.

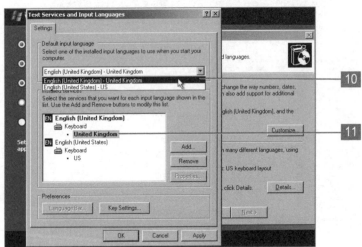

You will now get to enter your name, product code for your copy of Windows XP and some other details. If you've got an OEM version of Windows XP, the code should be on the plastic wrapper. If you bought a boxed copy, it'll be on the folder that the disk comes in. Ensure you get the code correct before pressing Enter, '8' and 'B' often get confused in the font Microsoft uses.

If you do enter the wrong code, you can just go back and correct it, a careful check will often reveal your mistake. Your XP code will never be shown to another user and is unique to your copy of Windows. It is also quite hard to find on the system so make sure you keep the original folder that it came in, safely.

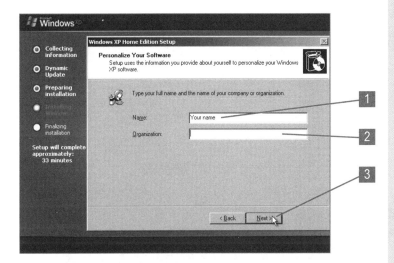

Entering important details

1 Enter your name in the space provided. It can be in any form you like but email programs will usually pick up on it for your actual name so you may want to keep it sensible.

2 If you're doing this for a business machine put the name of the company to whom it will belong. You can leave this blank if you want to or if you hate empty spaces then just fill it in with a personal name.

3 Press the Next button.

Jargon buster

Product code – most programs come with a product or license code. Without it you cannot complete the installation of your program. It is vital, therefore, that you take care not to lose the manual or disk case if this has the number printed on it. With Windows you will need to activate the program within 30 days of installation, either online or over the phone. This checks that your license is genuine.

6

Entering important details (cont.)

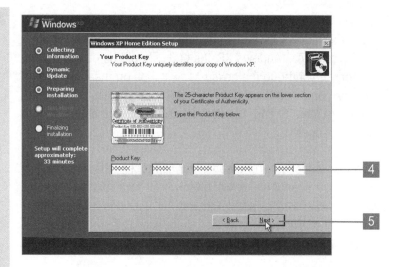

4. The product key will actually appear as it appears on your documentation. We've just XXXX'ed the lines out for illustrative purposes.

5. Once you're sure you've got the right key then click on the Next button.

6. You can now give your computer a name. Users of other computers on a network will see this, if you attach it to one. The default name is usually gibberish so at least give it something polite, even if you don't intend to network the computer.

For your information

Piracy of Windows is rife across the world and since counterfeit copies can look exactly like the real thing it is possible for copies to be sold as if they were original with no one being the wiser. If you have problems with your code that don't relate to mistaken entry, then check out this website to see if your copy is a real one: www.microsoft.com/resources/howtotell/en/office/faq.mspx

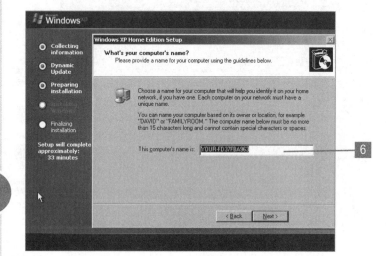

For your information

To confuse matters, any kind of data connection is called a network connection by Windows. A traditional local area network, however, functions differently to your modem or broadband internet and this name won't be seen online.

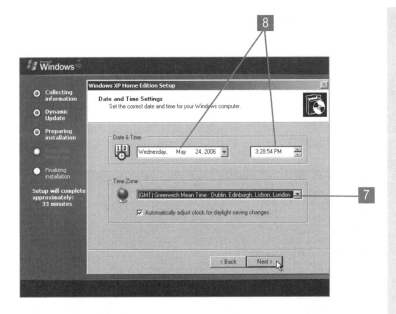

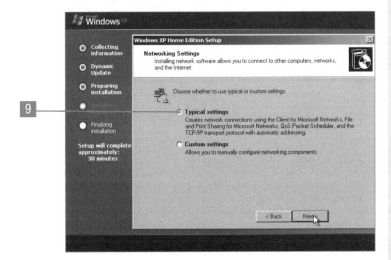

7 Windows defaults to an American time zone so ensure you set it to the correct British zone be it BST in the summer or GMT in the winter months.

8 You can also check that the time and date are correct. These are stored in the BIOS but you can change them from Windows at any time.

9 You'll set up your actual Internet connection once Windows has finished installing but you need to confirm your network settings now. Ensure Typical settings is selected unless you have a pressing need to mess about with the configuration. This will have nothing to do with any wireless networking so don't worry about that either.

Timesaver tip

Once Windows is installed you can click on the clock on the Start bar and take advantage of a feature to keep your system clock automatically up to date with an atomic clock connected to the Internet.

6

Entering important details (cont.)

10 Windows will now try to
create some more desktop
space to operate in by
increasing the screen
resolution a notch. This will
also test that the video driver
is working properly. Click OK.
The screen should go blank
for a few seconds and another
window will pop up to show
that the change has been
made. You can make your
own changes to the desktop
resolution and colour depth
later on.

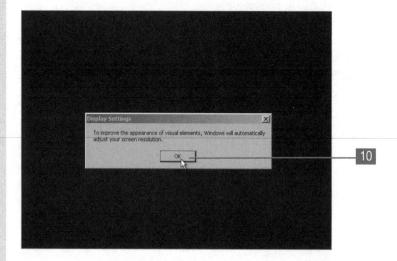

For your information

Modern video cards can display massive resolutions and
virtual desktops spread over a wider area than your
physical monitor, but you will need the full driver
package installed to use them rather than the basic XP
driver. This should be on a CD provided with the card, or
you can download the very latest version, and they are
updated regularly, from the web site.

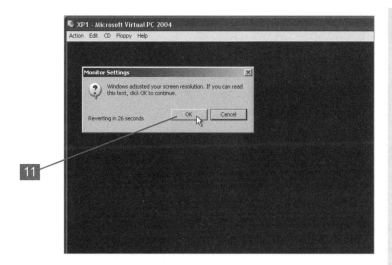

11 You will have 30 seconds to confirm that the screen change has taken place successfully. If you don't see this screen then the countdown will continue invisibly and if there is a problem it will revert to its working state once the timer has finished. In 99% of all cases you can click OK and continue on to the next step.

12 With these changes complete, Windows should now ask to restart and you should see the welcome sight of the 'Welcome' screen meaning that you've successfully installed Windows XP onto your new computer.

6

Configuring Windows XP for best performance

7

Introduction

Now you've got Windows XP installed on your system, you might think that things are cut and dried. However, there's a little way to go yet because the way XP is installed by default is never the best for any one system. For a start, there's a host of security settings to manage in order to ensure your computer stays free from attack while online.

Between the end of the last chapter and this one, you should have sorted out Internet access via your Internet Service Provider. Since there are so many of them we can't possibly cover all the ways of installing broadband or a modem and software; most ISP's have an install program on disk that does all the work for you anyway. Access to the online world is vital for a healthy system but also opens up your PC to the threats of viruses and worms that make for so many tabloid headlines.

You will want to install all the drivers for graphics and system performance, and change dozens of little settings in the Windows Registry to make your computer run smoothly. There are also lots of bits of Windows you can tune up or disable to eek out extra power.

This chapter will help you through all the, generally simple, changes that will see you getting the most from your system and show you how to access a host of powerful XP features that can make an average system run far faster than you'd think possible.

What you'll do

Secure and update Windows

Free anti-virus software

Free firewalls

Use automatic updates

Check your hardware

Update a driver

Jargon buster

Windows Registry – the power behind Windows is all in the Registry, a massive file that lists every piece of hardware and every system setting. It is read when the system starts up. Quite a few settings are worth changing to improve your system and improve stability. Over time, the registry can become clogged with old data, missing links and other errors that add to boot-up times and reduce system performance.

Securing and updating Windows

A few years back, every week brought a new scare story about worms, viruses and Trojans attacking Windows PCs. The reason there aren't so many headlines like this nowadays is that the majority of PCs are now better protected; mostly due to our sense of self-preservation but also thanks to initiatives like Microsoft Security Center. Windows XP from Service Pack 2 onwards comes with the minimum protection from viruses and hackers that the Internet can pose.

As Windows XP started for the first time you will have seen the front screen that informs you about automatic updates, virus protection and the Windows firewall. It probably warned you that you had no protection at all, but don't panic.

You may well already have your own virus and firewall software, so now is a good time to install these. Again there are too many options for us to cover in detail, but installing protection software is a similar routine to installing any other program. If they're recent editions, then the Security Center should recognise and monitor them for you.

If you don't have a virus checker then there are several that are almost as good as commercial software that you can download free from the Internet. In fact they are generally just cut-down versions of software that businesses pay for and offer free to individuals. All virus software today is updated daily to protect against the latest threats and you should get used to making sure the software is kept up to date.

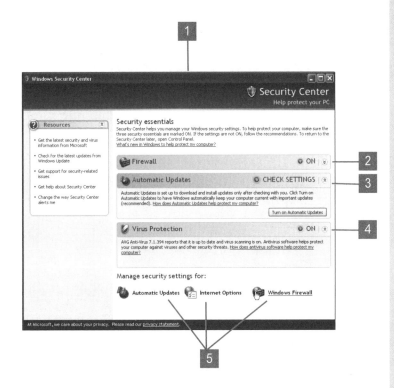

1 The standard Security Center screen will look something like this once your software is installed. The green lights are good, yellow means something needs checking and red lights mean you need to perform a task urgently.

2 The Firewall will certainly be on by default. If for some reason it isn't, turn it on. It will protect your PC from many online attacks.

3 You should have enabled Automatic Updates during Windows installation. If you didn't, it is worth doing so now to allow Windows to update itself with the latest protection fixes and patches as they are released.

4 If the Virus Protection section has an alarm next to it then you need to sort this out urgently. Either install your own software or download a free anti-virus utility (see Free anti-virus software).

5 To make changes to your security settings you can click one of these options to open up the appropriate toolbox. Select Windows Firewall.

Securing and updating Windows (cont.)

6 Left alone, the Internet Connection Firewall will happily protect your PC but it might also start blocking some information that you need to see. That's where the firewall options come into play. Click on the Exceptions tab.

7 A program or service with a tick next to it indicates that the Firewall will let through any information that program requires to send and receive. Sometimes when you install new software you may see a pop-up message that will give you the choice of either allowing it to connect to the Internet or to remain blocked by the firewall.

8 If you need to open a specific port, then you will have to specify it by clicking on the Add Port button and entering the details.

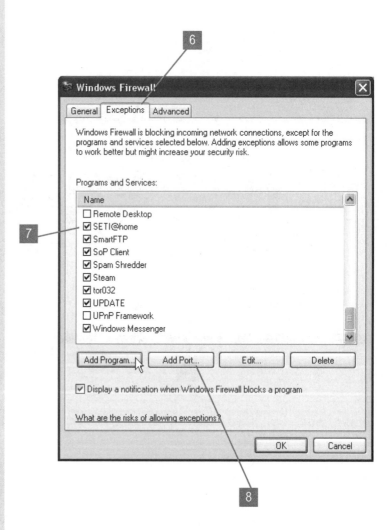

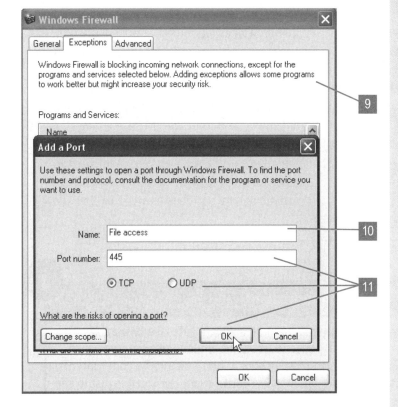

9 A port sometimes needs to be added when a program uses obscure or irregular port numbers. You'll see something is wrong when the program doesn't send or receive any data, in which case you'll need to find out from the program what the port number is.

10 Then enter a description for the port number in the Name box; ideally, either the name of the program that uses it or what the port does.

11 Enter the port number, choose the type of access it uses, and click OK to enable the port.

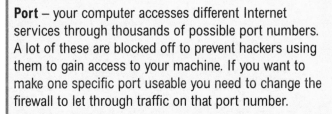

Jargon buster

Port – your computer accesses different Internet services through thousands of possible port numbers. A lot of these are blocked off to prevent hackers using them to gain access to your machine. If you want to make one specific port useable you need to change the firewall to let through traffic on that port number.

Free anti-virus software

There are several popular programs you can choose for virus protection that don't cost a penny. Personally, I use AVG Free Edition from http://free.grisoft.com. It comes with a shield that checks all programs and files you run for viruses, an email scanner and daily updates. You might also want to look at AntiVir PersonalEdition Classic, available from www.free-av.com/, or Free Avast! 4 Home Edition from www.avast.com. These will protect you against all the common viruses out there.

Windows Security Center comes with its own free firewall called Internet Connection Firewall (Windows Firewall). It's not the most feature-rich of programs but is reasonably effective at protecting your PC from attacks from the Internet, though not at all effective if a threat has already broken in. If you do have another firewall you can install, then all well and good. However, there are free alternatives you might want to download and try too! Since the Windows firewall is here you may as well use it for now.

For your information

If you read some comparative reviews you might find that free software gets less favourable reviews than software one has to pay for. My response to this criticism is to use the free online scanner from McAfee, one of the big names in virus protection, at http://uk.mcafee.com/root/mfs/default.asp called FreeScan. Use this to run a sweep on your system every few months just to see if it can pick up anything your free software might have missed. My free protection has never let me down but it never hurts to check.

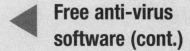
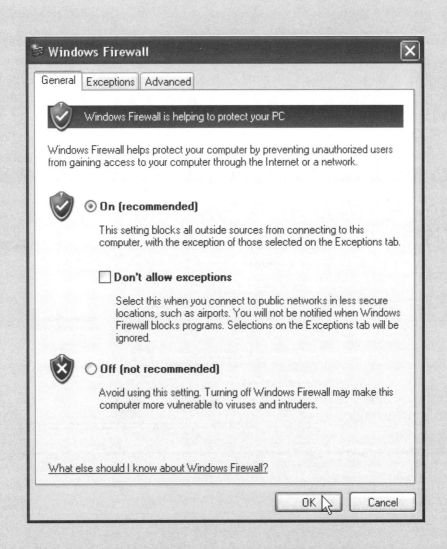

Important

If you want to install your own firewall software make sure you disable the Windows firewall first as firewalls do not work well together. They can clash and upset your Internet connection because they can see each other as threats. Most firewalls won't install with another running but it is always better to be safe than see your Internet connection vanish.

Free firewalls

Firewalls can earn their makers a lot of money so most 'free' versions are really cut-down variants of the one they like to sell you. Perhaps the most useful of these programs is Agnitum's Personal Firewall that can be found at www.agnitum.com/products/outpostfree/index.php. It features connection monitoring so you can see what comes and goes through the firewall and create rules to stop unwelcome visitors.

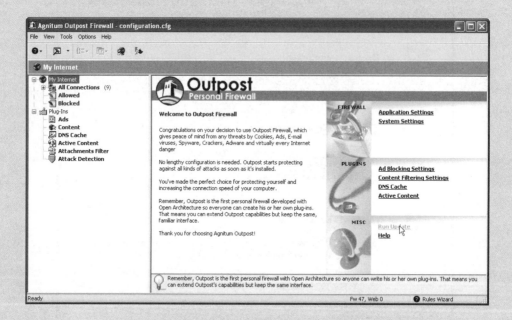

Automatic Updates make up a large part of the Security Center's operation. New patches, fixes and additional software are released for Windows on a daily basis, and vital updates are released monthly to make it easier for businesses to anticipate and incorporate them onto their systems.

When you get Windows up and running, the first thing it will try to do is use Windows Update to download them all for you. There could be an awful lot of them, so this is where we hope you have broadband.

Once that initial rush is over, Microsoft releases a batch of updates on the second Tuesday of every month; sometimes earlier if there is an especially critical problem. If you use Automatic Update proactively, or visit the Microsoft site, you can find plenty of other useful tools to grab for your system. To change the way they work, go through Security Center and click on the Automatic Updates button at the bottom of the screen.

1 To read more about automatic updates and why they are so important to Windows, click on the link in the main tab.

2 To change the settings, click on Automatic Updates at the bottom of the window.

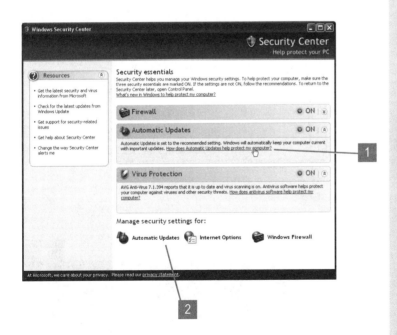

i

For your information

Quite a few programs, drivers and utilities like to check for updates automatically. This trend means you're less likely to spot updates occurring. If you want to keep control of your system, always make sure a program tells you before it updates. Often this option is found in the settings for the particular program such as QuickTime. Many others do this.

Using automatic updates (cont.)

3 The recommended setting will let Windows download and install updates on a daily basis. You can choose the time and set the process to occur once a week on a specified day if you wish.

4 The second option will let the system download your updates but will ask you first if it's okay to install them. This is a smart compromise for people who want to know exactly what goes onto their system. It provides a useful pause in case one update causes problems with Windows or other programs. These are usually reported within minutes of the problem happening and, if you hear about it quickly enough, you can choose not to install the problematic update.

5 The Notify me ... option gives you complete control over what is downloaded and installed onto your machine and is more useful with something like a server where what goes onto the system can be critical.

6 Turning off Automatic Updates stops your system being updated and means you'll have to go to the Updates website to find and download new patches.

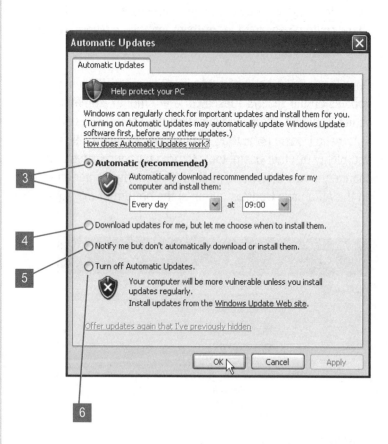

Important

When you've installed a batch of updates it is strongly recommended that you restart the computer there and then when prompted rather than carry on working. This means all the changes will be completed and you can continue in safety.

Using automatic
updates (cont.)

7

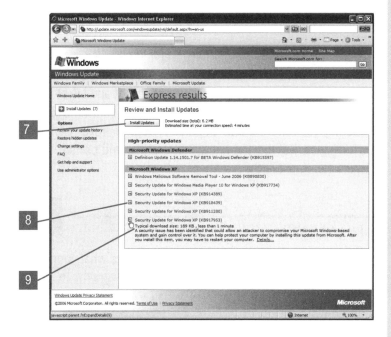

7 Sometimes you'll hear about updates being made available before your machine checks automatically for them. You can download and install them manually from the Update site http://update.microsoft.com/ windowsupdate. This applies too if you've turned off Automatic Update. Click here to install the selected latest updates to your system.

8 You can read about what each update affects by clicking on the '+' box.

9 The estimated time to download the updates is given here.

10 When you start the download process you'll see the progress of downloading and installing each update here.

11 This bar highlights the progress of the downloading process.

12 If you need to cancel any updates, you can do them later just by rerunning the Updates web page.

Configuring Windows XP for best performance 109

Checking your hardware

1. Go to the Start menu and click on the Control Panel option to display this window.

2. If you see the window entitled Pick a category, click the Switch to Classic View option on the left-hand side of the Control Panel window to make it easier to access.

With Windows now installed, secure and updated, you can check that all of your hardware is working properly using the Device Manager, a feature of the Control Panel. Every bit of hardware has its own driver; from the mouse and keyboard to the display, they were either installed automatically by Windows or came on disk with the component. Updated drivers also have been downloaded in the background.

In some cases, XP might not have 'seen' the hardware at all, or it may have installed a generic or outdated driver, so it is well worth your time investigating. Getting the right and latest driver may add more speed and features to some of your hardware. Hopefully you're aware that graphics drivers improve performance. But did you know that scanner and printer drivers can improve the quality of results?

Jargon buster

Driver – this is a piece of code that describes what your hardware can do and tells the PC and Windows how to talk to it. Drivers can also include their own programs, allowing you to enable features and adjust settings on that item of hardware.

3

4

3 You should now see the regular Control Panel in a more accessible form; double-click on the System icon.

4 Now click on the Hardware tab at the top of the new window. This will show another window that gives three options, of which we want the top one.

For your information

The Control Panel provides access to most of the hardware and system elements of your computer from the network adapter to your Internet settings. If you're not familiar with it, taking a tour through the icons will teach you a lot about how your computer works. Most of the setting changes you can make are obvious but be sure you know what you're changing before doing anything too technical.

Configuring Windows XP for best performance 111

Checking your hardware (cont.)

5 Device Manager is what we are after. Double-click this to open a new Window that shows all your hardware components on the system.

6 Driver Signing is a system that proves your drivers are approved for XP.

7 If you need another way to access Windows Update you can do it from here.

Jargon buster

Driver signing – a signed driver is one that has been approved for use by Microsoft for Windows XP. This means that it has gone through all their quality checks. Often, new drivers aren't signed because it can take months for one to be checked, so don't worry if you get messages saying that your driver isn't signed. It is more a political statement than a matter of concern as the majority of hardware companies do plenty of testing to ensure their driver works properly.

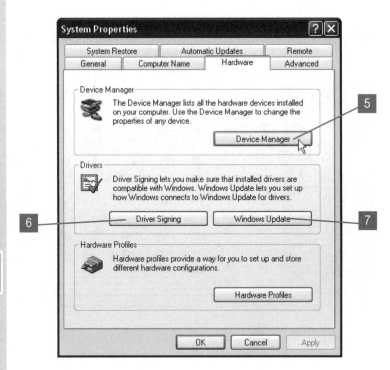

For your information

On your first visit to Device Manager it's worth having a browse through all the sections so that you learn what goes where and can establish that all components are at least recognised by the system.

8 When using Device Manager you'll see a sizeable list of components broken down into sections with the name of your computer at the top. Each section can cover one or several parts, usually grouped in a logical fashion.

9 Use the '+' boxes to expand a section and find more details.

10 Conversely, use the '-' boxes to hide them again as the list can get unwieldy with everything open.

For your information

Non-working hardware, or hardware for which no driver has been found, is listed at the bottom of the Device Manager list. As you've just installed a brand new PC it is more than possible that there are one or two components that weren't correctly detected. These could include RAID disk management (something that most systems have these days but very few people make use of) or audio drivers which you'll definitely be wanting. In some very rare cases you might see an entry for unknown hardware; something that is a complete mystery to the system. If you see a piece of hardware not working that you would prefer to function, there are two ways of going about getting it up and running: The first is, find the correct driver. It is most likely to be on the CD that came with the motherboard if it's a component you didn't add yourself. The second is to let Windows try and find the right driver by following the steps below.

Updating a driver

Some drivers are installed simply by putting the CD that came with the hardware in the drive. A program will automatically start and install the driver for you. If the driver came on a floppy disk, or you don't have a driver for the piece of hardware, then you can go through the Hardware Update Wizard.

There are then a series of options you can choose to install the driver depending on where it is. You can also let XP search for the latest driver. This is probably one of my least favourite parts of Windows in terms of annoyance and lack of clarity, but it is essential for getting the best drivers installed for some of your components.

1 The Hardware Update Wizard is launched by right-clicking on any piece of hardware in the Device Manager and choosing the Update Driver ... option.

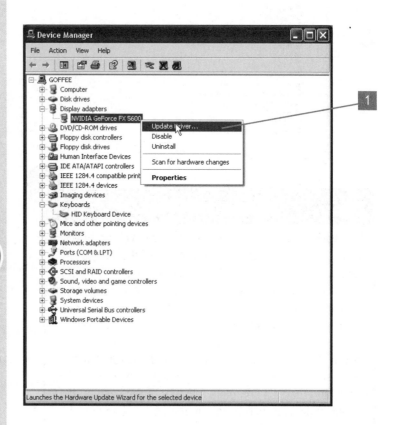

For your information

If you're having trouble finding a driver for a particular piece of hardware, there are several sites on the web that can help out. Both www.windrivers.com and www.nodevice.com charge a subscription fee. If that's a bit off putting you can generally drag up a driver by searching for the specific model through Yahoo! or Google.

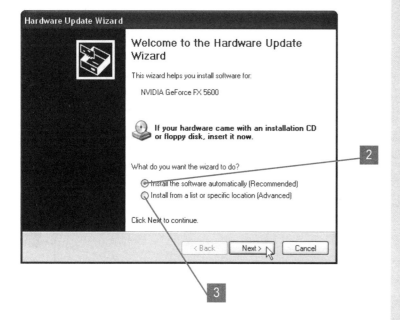

2 The next screen gives you two choices to help narrow down your options. At this point if you have the driver on a CD then you'll want to pop it in the drive. If you don't have a driver or don't know where to find one then the first option is your best choice.

3 If you have the driver on a disk or copied to your hard disk, then you might want to choose this so you can tell Windows exactly where to find it rather than go on a lengthy search.

Updating a driver (cont.)

4 If you chose the Let Windows Search option it will check in a range of places for the latest driver.

5 Once it finds a driver it'll start to download the files and install them automatically for you.

6 Once the installation is complete, you can restart the computer and the job will be completed rather painlessly. If only all driver installations went like this.

Timesaver tip

When Windows has completed the task successfully, restart the computer for the update to complete and for all features of the driver to be activated. As a rule, restart your machine after each hardware change just to make certain that each update works correctly rather than change a number of drivers and then try to figure out which one is causing a problem.

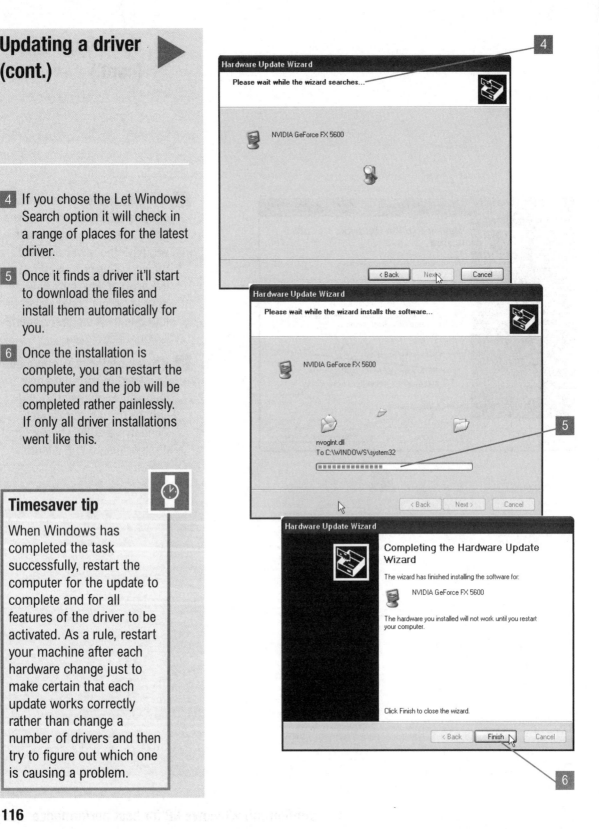

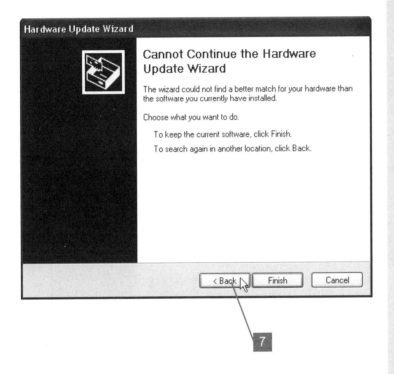

7 If Windows can't find a driver either on your system or from an online source then it will complete the wizard without success. If you do have a new driver to hand then you might want to go back and try some of the different options of the wizard, particularly the Install from a list or specific location to guide Windows in the right direction.

For your information

Some drivers come as executable files that you run just like programs. To confuse things further, they often come with a bundle of utilities or programs that install at the same time. Even more confusing, Microsoft, Logitech and others who produce keyboard and mice bundles often just have the one driver for a whole range of products. The best places to search for a driver are on the official product website, then the main company site and, finally, on general hardware web sites.

Updating a driver (cont.) ▶

8　You can choose where the installer will look to find the driver. If it's on CD then you only need tick that box to keep down the time it takes for the computer to find the driver.

9　When you click Next, Windows should track down the driver you've indicated and install it for you.

10　Windows XP has a host of drivers listed by default. You can also browse through their list to see if your hardware is located there.

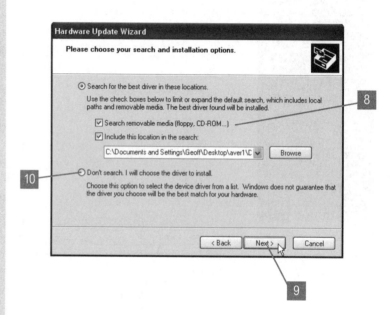

Timesaver tip

As more hardware utilities become online-aware, they will often check for the latest drivers and other updates themselves. If your hardware has this feature then it can save you time and effort tracking down drivers. It also means that you get the latest features for your hardware efficiently and quickly.

Benchmarking and overclocking

8

Introduction

Once Windows is finally properly installed and ready to go, you can start filling that neat, roomy, hard disk with all your favourite programs and games. However, may we suggest you hold off for a little while and do some testing first just to find out how good your system really is.

Benchmarking is a popular PC hobby in its own right for gamers, upgraders and people who've just built their own system. The simple idea is that you test your machine using a few standard programs and then compare the results online against others with similar systems. From the results you can see what performance tweaks could be made, and what a little extra power in the graphics, memory or processor department could do. Two systems may be similar in specification but rarely do they produce the same results. By using comparisons you can find out where your system could do with a little boost.

The practical benefits of benchmarking are far reaching. If you see a result that is much below expectation then you'll know something isn't quite right. There could be a BIOS setting running below what your system is capable of, or a resource hog dragging down your system speed. You might also find a few simple over-clocking processes can eek out a little extra power from your computer for free.

What you'll do

Download and install Futuremark programs

Test your system with PC Mark

Test your system with 3D Mark

Overclock your video card

Benchmarking has almost become a sport among computer enthusiasts. Using the forums you can discuss tips and tactics for building a better system or find out which components provide great power at a decent price and which should be avoided at all costs.

Futuremark has long been the leading creator of benchmarking programs for the PC enthusiast. By tying the software into an online results database and forum, where people can find out about others' results and discuss how to get better performance, it has built a massive following. The company's two leading programs are PC Mark, which tests the whole system, and 3D Mark which stresses the video card.

You can get the latest versions of each program from the Futuremark site at www.futuremark.com. There are free trial versions you can use but buying the full version of each program gets you extra features and tests. The free version is more than enough for our purposes.

PC Mark is aimed at a wide range of systems while 3D Mark is very much for those with the latest graphics cards. Therefore, unless you spent a hefty part of your budget on a top-end video card it might not be something you'll get too much from.

For your information

Futuremark's programs aren't the only benchmarking tools out there. You might want to give SiSoftware's Sandra 2007 a try, This features a massive battery of tests for a very thorough interrogation of your system; it's available at www.jaggedonline.com.

You can also find some useful free, small and quick-to-download tools like Video Card Stability Test from http://freestone-group.com/ and Performance Test 6.0 from www.passmark.com/.

Downloading and installing Futuremark programs

8

Downloading and installing Futuremark programs (cont.)

1 Point your web browser at the Futuremark site www.futuremark.com and wait for their shiny home page to load.

2 Click on the Products section to head directly to the page with a handy list of all their products.

3 Futuremark has a range of programs, but from this list we want to download one or both of 3D Mark and PC Mark. Both programs get regular updates but at the time of writing we're up to PC Mark 05 and 3D Mark 06.

4 The 3D Mark download link will take you straight to a referring page that will provide you with a list of download links.

5 If you want to buy a copy of PC Mark or 3D Mark over the web, click the purchase link at the bottom of each item.

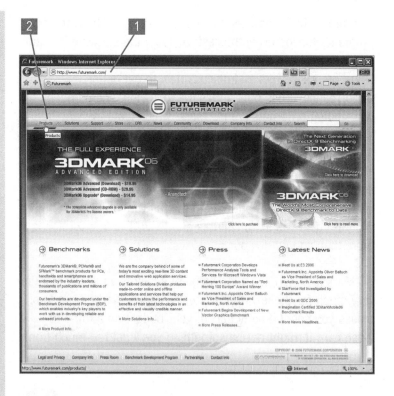

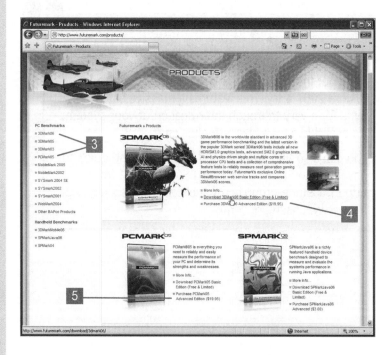

For your information

Futuremark came to fame under their former name Mad Onion when they developed one of the first really popular benchmarking tools for the growing generation of fast 3D graphics cards for PCs. Over successive generations their tests became more graphically detailed and more taxing. They are used by most hardware reviewers to help find out which systems and cards are the best.

6 Check your system against the requirements list before downloading the massive 580 MB 3D Mark file. It would be a shame to get it only to find you couldn't run it at all. PC Mark has less aggressive system requirements.

7 At the bottom of the page will be a list of links from where you can download the program. Choose one located reasonably near to you if possible.

8 Click the Download button to head over to the best site to get the file from. Then repeat the process for the other program.

8

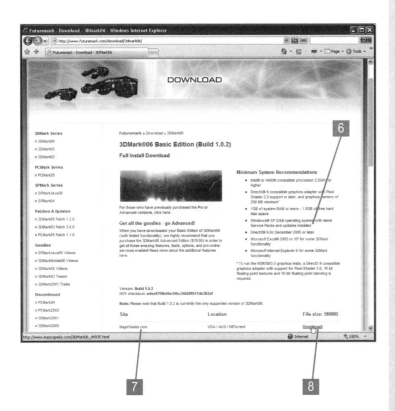

Downloading and installing Futuremark programs (cont.)

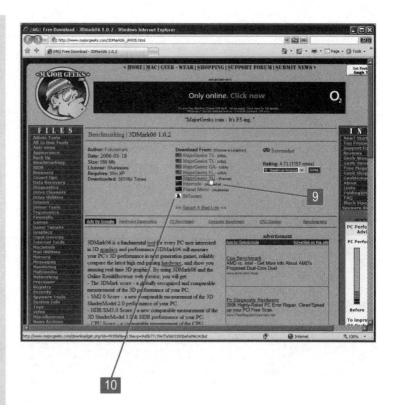

9 Most file sites provide another list of links to ensure you get the file from a server as close as possible to you.

10 BitTorrent is a useful service that distributes the task of downloading files from a single server to all the machines that have downloaded the file from it. Click the Torrent link if you have a BitTorrent client installed.

Jargon buster

BitTorrent – peer-to-peer file sharing allows your computer to grab parts of a file from any computer that has it and is sharing it. This takes the load off a single server, where thousands of people could be trying to get a file at any one time, and distributes it around the web. You need to download a BitTorrent client before you can receive files in this way. Try www.bittorrent.com/ and select "Get the BitTorrent Client" under BitTorrent Tools.

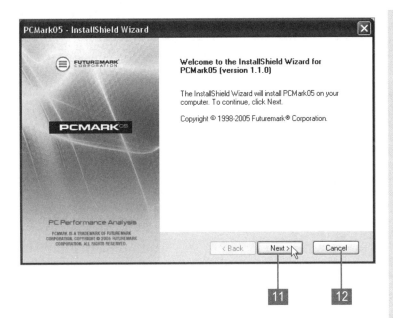

8

11 Once the download has completed, double-click the icon and then click Next to install the program.

12 If you don't want to install the program right now, click Cancel.

13 As with most pieces of software you need to sign up to the license agreement before it will even let you install the program. Click the I Accept option to enable the Next button.

14 If you really want to read one of these documents it's a lot easier to print it out and read it on paper.

15 When you're ready, click the Next button to continue.

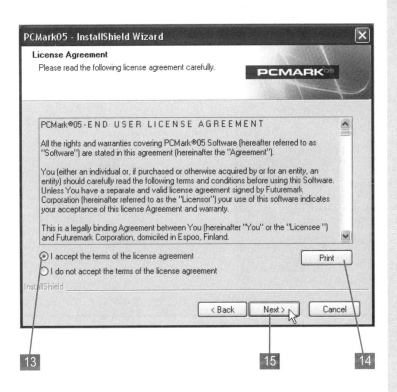

Downloading and installing Futuremark programs (cont.)

16 You'll need a credit card to buy the program online. This method gives you immediate access to the product.

17 If you bought the product online you'll have received an email with the registration code that you'll need to enter here.

18 If you just want to use the program for free, click the Purchase Later button, this doesn't mean that it will force you to buy at a later time.

19 For once, I strongly recommend you make sure the View Readme button is ticked as there is important information for both Futuremark programs that needs to be checked out.

20 Decide if you really want another icon on the desktop.

21 Click the Finish button.

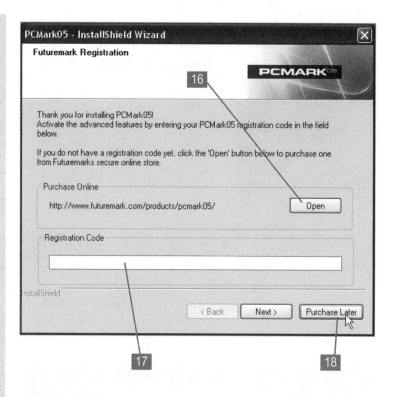

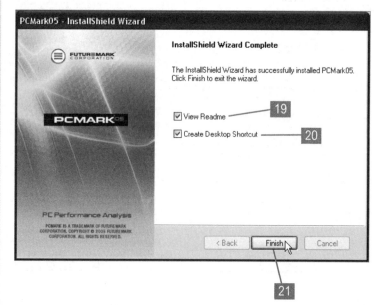

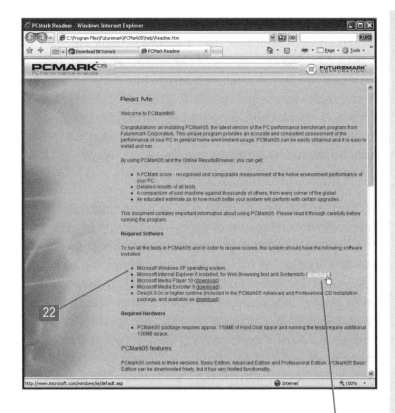

Downloading and installing Futuremark programs (cont.)

8

22 In the documentation you'll find that some extra software needs to be installed to ensure that PC Mark runs smoothly.

23 Click the Download button to go straight to the right place for any files that you don't have. Some Futuremark programs won't run without them.

Testing your system with PC Mark

1 The tests can be customised if you buy the full version, but for now you are limited to running the main tests in a fixed sequence.

2 You'll see the main specification of your system listed here and can check out the nuts and bolts by clicking on the Details button.

3 When you've finished a test sequence the results will pop up here and can be analysed in depth.

4 Click the Run PC Mark button to start the tests. Ensure that all other programs are closed down before you start.

PC Mark runs a batch of different sub-programs that stress the main parts of the computer by throwing lots of data at them, making the processor do lots of calculations and other tricks, to bring it to a halt. The rationale behind this digital torture is to find weak spots in the system so that you can fix them with a tweak or upgrade. The program can even suggest what needs fixing so it's ideal for the newcomer to PC tweaking. Batches of tests can be run automatically and the results will pop out at the end.

PC Mark isn't as visually thrilling as its larger brother but it does a more thorough test of the system, helping to track down bottlenecks that might impede your PC from running as well as it should. The full version of the program can be highly customised. In the free edition, however, you pretty much just press the Test button and let the system get on with thrashing away at your RAM, processor, hard disk and graphics card with a series of intensive tests including video encoding and animation. When it's finished you can check your scores against anyone else who has registered online. That way you get to figure out how to beat their scores.

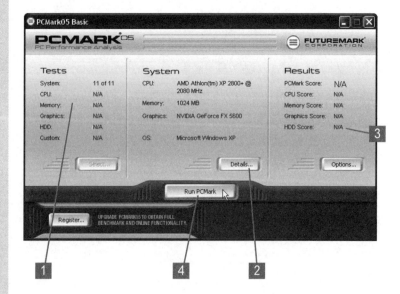

Important

To get a valid benchmark score it is important that you run your system on an even footing with those of other users. This generally means that no other non-essential programs are running, even those that live in the task tray. For best practice you should also restart your PC before each run and, if you're being really thorough, you should run the tests three times and take the average score.

5 The test screen shows all the benchmarks in progress. Don't press a key or move the mouse. Even that could affect the scores or cause the process to be aborted.

6 If a benchmark run aborts then it could be because something else is running. Check that all programs are closed and start again.

7 If you do want to stop a run of tests, just click the Abort button.

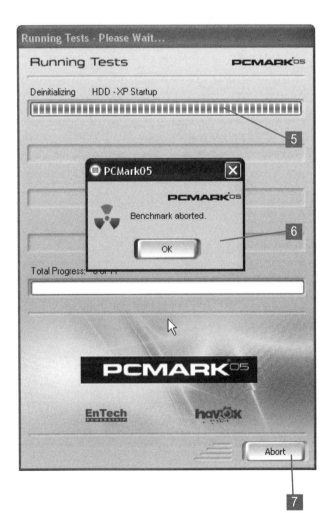

Testing your system with PC Mark (cont.)

8 When the tests are finished you'll see your results score here. The figure itself is meaningless in isolation so you'll need to find something to compare it with.

9 If you want to check out the details of the score, click Details. Ideally this should be done once you've done a few test runs and have a number of results to compare.

10 For an online check as to how good your score is, click Online ResultBrowser or ORB.

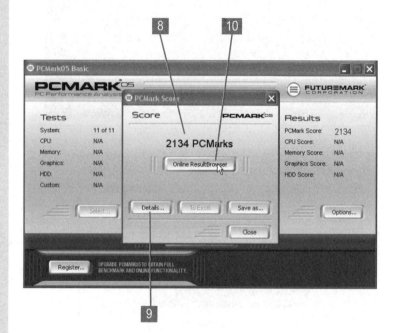

For your information

You'll need to register to use Online ResultBrowser, but it is free. All you need provide is an email address and password. Then you can use it to compare your score and system with thousands of other users' scores.

8

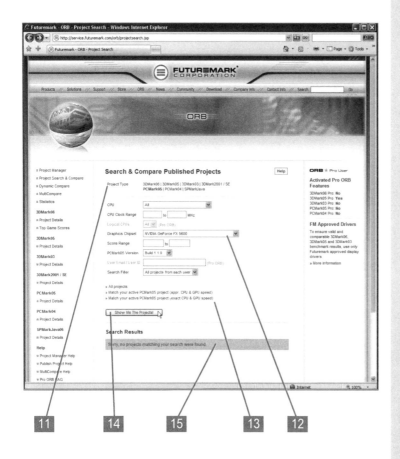

11 Once logged into the ORB, make sure you choose the right Project Type from this list. Otherwise you'll be comparing entirely different programs.

12 Choose what it is you want to compare your results with. You might want to look at systems with the same graphics card as yours to see what difference an alternate processor might make; or perhaps the opposite.

13 To avoid making any choices yourself, click one of the Match your active PCMark 05 Project buttons to see your score compared with roughly equivalent or identical systems.

14 When you're sorted, click Show Me The Projects to start comparing.

15 If no projects match then you'll see this line and should widen your search criteria to find something to compare with.

Testing your system with PC Mark (cont.)

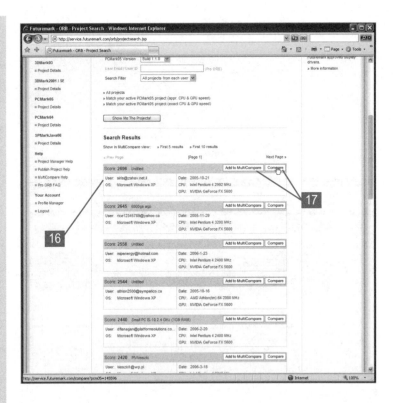

16 Each result appears with the score listed first and the processor and graphics card details in the information box.

17 To compare a system with your own, click the Compare button or you can add more than one by using the MultiCompare button.

18 The detailed comparison shows a long list of stats and results for your system's performance coupled with those of another system.

19 Scroll up and down to find out the areas where systems differ, if there's a huge difference you can start to figure out why it happened.

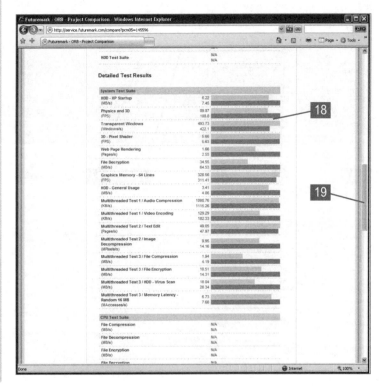

3D Mark 2006 is the current standard for stressing the latest video cards to see just how good or bad your system's performance is. It is designed really to make the latest gaming systems struggle, so we don't recommend you get your hopes up for an amazing score if you've put together a neat little system. The process follows roughly the same format as the PC Mark system of tests. Follow those steps for installing and getting the program running. Again if you buy the complete version you get more features and tests to play with.

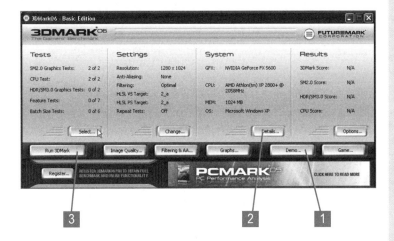

1. When clicked, most of the buttons show a link to the full version only. You can still run the demo and the benchmarks.

2. To find out some incredibly in-depth details of your graphics card and system click the Details button in the System box.

3. Click on Run 3DMark to start the series of tests.

8

For your information

If your budget card isn't really up to handling the power that the latest 3D Mark generates, you can still download earlier versions back to the year 2001 from shareware sites like www.tucows.com and others. This will let you get a measurement of performance that you will be able to compare with other machines because the ORB still records all these tests.

Testing your system with 3D Mark (cont.)

4 Each test takes a short time to load. The first time you start the program it will take a couple of minutes to unpack all the files.

5 Visual detail and stunning effects are key to the program testing your hardware to its limits. The frame rate is the number of images your computer can get to the screen per second. An ideal modern system should manage at least 30 frames per second.

6 At the end of the test you get an overall score.

7 You can look at the individual scores per test; ideal if you're looking for a specific weakness in your system.

8 Most of the fun with Futuremark products is comparing your score against others using Online ResultBrowser.

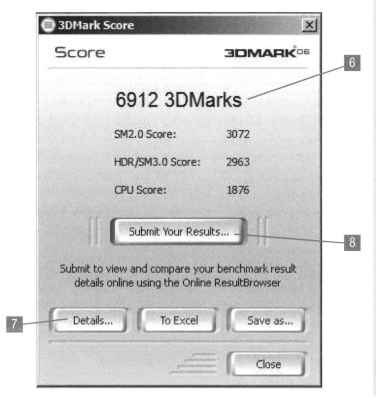

Overclocking your video card

One thing many people notice when comparing one system with a similar one, is that their benchmark scores are beaten because other users have overclocked graphics cards. In some cases the maker of the card might have done this. Several companies sell cards running faster than their original rating; hopefully, with some improved cooling installed as faster operation generates more heat. Or the user may have done it themselves with a small software utility that you can download or will find as part of the driver.

For the video card user, mostly gamers and hardware enthusiasts, it started out as a highly informal technique of speeding up the graphics processor and its memory. This was risky stuff a few years ago but is now so standard that most graphics card makers supply utilities with their drivers to help you do it with ease and in safety.

Your graphics card and its memory are supposed to run at, say, 400 MHz. You can use the overclocking, utility to increase the core and memory speed by small increments, say 5 MHz a go to start with. Then test the card out with your favourite game to make sure the speed increase doesn't make the card run unstably. Next, run your benchmark program to find out the practical effect of the speed increase.

Thereafter, increase your overclocked speed another step and see what results that brings. Keep on pushing the speed up. At some point either the graphics in your game will start showing strange tears in the display or it will lock up completely. This is because it is running just too fast for your hardware or the heat has got too much and has triggered an automatic shut down. You may find that at the maximum safe overclocked speed you are able to get an extra 10 to 20% or even more performance from your card without having to pay for it.

ATI Cards come with a set of drivers called Catalyst. These are updated on a regular basis. Nvidia powered graphics cards use software called ForceWare drivers. As a part of the package, there is a program called nTune that you might need to download separately from the Nvidia website at www.nvidia.co.uk.

Jargon buster

Overclocking – this refers to the technique of changing the speed of your CPU, graphics chip or memory to improve computer performance. This is possible because the actual speed of every chip made is slightly different. They are put together by approximate speed rating and marketed as running at a particular rate. However, the speed of each chip can be increased a little, or a lot, by changing BIOS settings or installing special software.

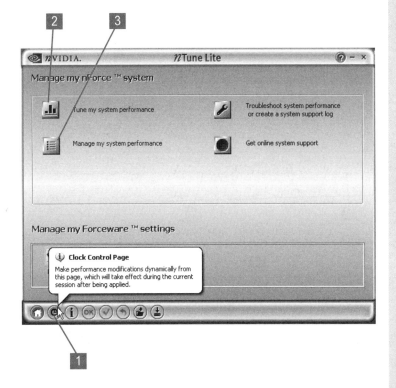

8

1 Once nTune has started
running you need to click the
second icon from the left on
the bottom row to access the
main overclocking controls.

2 The tuning system gives you
three levels of automatic
performance boosts to help
get the most from your
system. It can take from 20
minutes to an hour to test and
install.

3 If you choose the Manage my
system performance option
then nTune will offer to
automatically manage
performance.

For your information

If you don't have a NVIDIA
or an ATI powered graphics
card then you should still be
able to find a tuner program
for your chipset; a search on
the web for 'Matrox
overclock tool' or whatever
the name of your graphics
system is called should
produce results.

Benchmarking and overclocking 137

Overclocking your video card (cont.)

4 Hold the cursor over an area of the screen to get more information about what it does.

5 The GPU bus speed sliders will change the performance levels at which your graphics card works.

6 Memory controller timings are best left alone unless you're feeling particularly brave.

7 System bus speed changes affect the speed at which the motherboard communications work.

8 To increase the speed at which a part of the system runs, drag the slider to the right slightly. You'll need to test each step to ensure stability before using it permanently.

9 Use the save and load icons at the bottom to keep various settings that you may want to use on a regular basis.

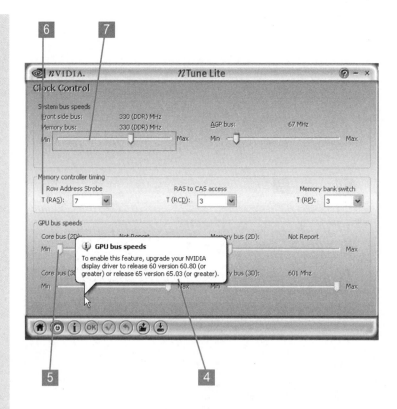

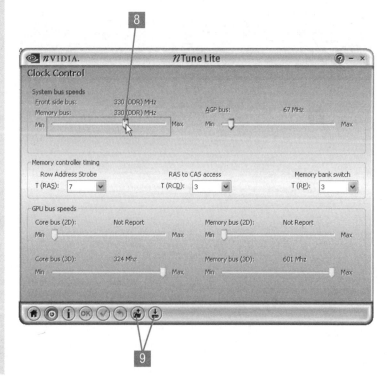

Expanding your PC

9

Introduction

Now all is well with your new system. It's ready to be put to work, be it playing games, video or photo work, surfing the net or office use. Whatever you use it for, particularly if it's either of the first two examples, we bet it won't be long before you're looking for a bit of an upgrade. In this section we take a look at the art of computer expansion, something that can boost your PC in ways with which overclocking, can't help.

No task, from the simplicity of a new hard drive to a full computer transplant, will hold any fear for you now that you've built your own PC. There are two main reasons to improve your system with an upgrade; for performance and for aesthetics. Be it more storage or power, PCs never really stand still. You can join the army of happy upgraders who keep their boxes up with the times and never worry about having to buy another whole system. For you aesthetes it's possible to make your PC run more quietly or even silently, which is very desirable in the confines of a quiet house. Or, you might want to turn your PC into an object of attention with flashing lights, neon tubes, designer touches and more.

Power upgraders concentrate on three main areas: additional memory or storage space; power through a processor or graphics card upgrade; and other areas such as audio or a monitor upgrade for more desktop space. The simplest way to upgrade the PC is through external additions. Upgrading a monitor is the simplest of them all. Adding an external hard disk drive rather than bolting another one into the case adds portability to your data, something that might come in useful.

What you'll do

Upgrade your memory

Upgrade your graphics card

Upgrade your cooling

Upgrade your processor

Add case lighting

Upgrade your display

Create a wireless network

Add extra features

Jargon buster

Power upgraders – what might start out as a couple of little tweaks can rapidly develop into a full blown hobby. Power upgraders live on the cutting edge of PC technology, always buying the latest and fastest gear, which they overclock to the maximum speed, to keep their PC running as fast as possible.

For your information

Upgrading your system one component at a time makes it easier to get the best possible price and performance as you're only concerned with a single item. You'll also know compatibility issues and restrictions in advance. As with buying the parts for your original PC, the more time you can spend doing research the more knowledgeable you'll be when coming to a buying decision.

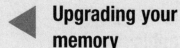

Adding memory is one of the simpler and most effective ways of improving PC performance. In simple terms, the more memory you have the less time the PC spends looking at the hard disk and, since memory is many times faster than a hard disk, the less time your system will take to perform a task. The minimum specification for memory is 512 MB but most systems come with 1 GB and you'll soon find 2 GB will be the standard allocation when Windows Vista becomes the mainstream operating system.

There are two ways to upgrade your memory. You can complement your existing RAM with more of the same (e.g. double up on a single 512 MB stick to give a total of 1 GB); or, if your memory slots are full of low capacity memory (say two 256 MB sticks) replace them with two 1 GB sticks to seriously boost your computing power. It all depends on the number of memory slots and what you have in them as to what approach you take. You can also buy faster memory if your motherboard is compatible so you get an extra speed boost when it is installed.

Upgrading your graphics card

Video power generates more sales than almost anything else in PC stores as the card and graphics-chip makers release new, improved models at least twice a year. However, the cost of a new video card is prohibitive to most of us. So, when a new range comes out, most of us look for the previous fastest models to come down in price to a reasonable level. There are three grades of video card. The cheapest borrow your system's memory rather than use their own. Next up the line are consumer cards which have most of the features of the enthusiast cards but trimmed down a little. Enthusiast cards now come for around £350 and are the cutting edge

cards. They can even be bought in pairs and run together on some motherboards for extreme gaming performance.

If your machine has an AGP graphics slot on the motherboard, you may struggle to upgrade it to the latest cards as these are almost all PCI-X type cards. A few do come out in AGP form but you'll be hard pressed to get hold of one. Not only do new cards have faster chips and more impressive visual features but they will most likely come with more memory too, allowing games to run at higher resolutions on screen and, thereby, adding more detail to the gaming experience.

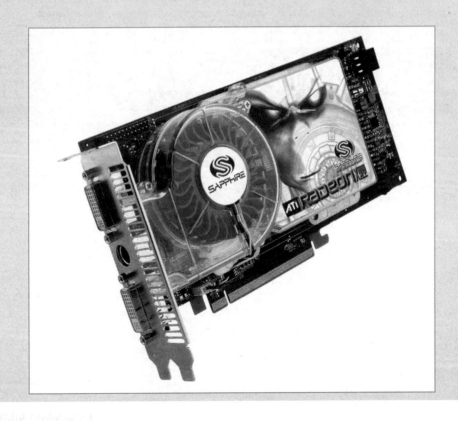

Upgrading your cooling

If you want your system to run a little quieter and cooler then there are many solutions out there to help. Extra fans can be bought that attach to the case and will reduce the temperature inside the system by improving airflow. They are a cheap and quick solution if you find your PC running too hot for comfort.

Going for a quieter system offers up several possible solutions. Firstly, you can buy exotic heatsinks that cut out the need for the main fan. Others allow a larger fan that rotates relatively slowly and is therefore less noisy.

At the extreme end of upgrading the thermal protection for your PC is the seemingly insane idea of water cooling. Water and computers don't mix so you need to be very sure of what you're doing to add a system that pumps water across the processor – and, optionally, the graphics chip – to remove the heat. With only the sound of a small pump, your PC will be a far quieter beast to work next to.

Upgrading your processor

Assuming you purchased a reasonably modern motherboard, you'll be able to keep up with the latest processors for some time to come. All you need do is unclip the old one (and maybe sell it on eBay to recoup some investment), then insert the new one. Add new thermal paste, re-attach the cooler, and away you go with a faster running system. With dual core chips, effectively two processors in the one box, becoming dramatically cheaper this year and quad core chips appearing by 2008 the power of the processor in your computer is about to rocket. Having the right motherboard could see you take advantage of that power when the new chips are released without having to buy a whole new system.

With transparent sides appearing on many cases it is increasingly popular to have a spooky or electric glow provided by a simple cool neon tube lurking under your desk. These lights are easily connected to the power supply through one of the spare drive plugs and can be stuck almost anywhere around the edge of a case. The effect can range from the subtle to the garish depending on the tastes of the owner but it does add an interesting element and gets away from the old idea of the PC being a desktop monolith.

Fans with lights add an extra element to the look of a case. If you visit the right store you can find almost any piece of hardware with some interesting looking modification to turn the PC into a system worthy of respect.

While most of these delightful gizmos appeal to gamers and hardcore modders, there is definitely a case for even the most conservative of PC users adding just a little extra something to make their system stand out from the crowd.

Jargon buster

Modders – the term describes PC enthusiasts who, while often interested in speed, are really into making their idea of the best looking PC. Some modded systems are truly things of beauty and design while others are just mad collections of neon lights. Some modders spend many times the value of a basic PC on a custom or homebuilt case and accessories.

Upgrading your display

With televisions and movies about to enter the high-definition age, it is interesting to note that most monitors larger than 15" are already capable of showing Hi-Def content. However, in the next year or so we'll see graphics cards with a new type of connector that encrypts the data of Hi-Def content to prevent it being copied and pirated. You'll obviously need a new monitor to make use of this feature so expect Hi-Def content to stop working on your existing monitor fairly soon. Hi-Def movies will also come on either Blu-Ray or HD-DVD discs, a problem you'll have to solve by choosing one format and sticking to it, buying both drives, or waiting for the release of combo drives that read both.

The big force behind monitor upgrades is switching from bulky, heavy and costly CRT screens to cheaper, space-efficient LCD screens that take up far less space on the desktop or can be bolted to the wall.

There's also the improvement of space on the desktop; a 15" screen offers 1024×728 resolution while a 17" screen can manage 1280×1024, and anything bigger should be fine for 1600×1200, which is big enough for any application.

Increasingly, people have more than one computer in the home and only one phone line or broadband Internet connection. This means either having a tangle of wires around the home or adopting the modern solution of a wireless network.

Wireless, generally called Wi-Fi, allows computers to share an Internet connection just as if they were running on a standard network. The main computer needs a wireless router connected to it. Most consumer models are broadband routers that sit between the PC and the Internet connection which is then shared with any other PC over the airwaves. Each remote PC, be it in the office or bedroom, connects using a Wi-Fi adapter. Most laptops have these built in but a simple USB stick is the easiest solution for a desktop PC.

9

With a broadband router, you share your internet access with the rest of the house. Using a password will prevent anyone lurking outside or in the same block of flats from stealing your bandwidth, while encryption will stop the casual hacker from reading what data leaks out through the walls.

Jargon buster

Wi-Fi – is a standard set of protocols that allow computers to talk using radio waves. In the home, this is ideal for sharing an Internet connection between computers in different rooms. Wi-Fi hotspots in public places such as designated coffee shops and libraries allow anyone using a laptop to access the Internet without worrying about plugging in or changing complicated settings.

For your information

If you don't like the idea of your data flying through the air for others to inspect, nor the ugly wiring of a traditional network, then you can use a system from Devolo that sends your data around the mains wiring. All you have is one network lead connected to a special box that plugs into the mains with another such box in a second room and a network lead from that to your second PC.

Adding extra features

This could really be called the odds and sods area of upgrading. There are all kinds of widgets that you can stick on the modern PC. Examples include a media card reader, ideal for pulling photos off your digital camera, and a USB powered coffee cup warmer.

Card readers can be either external USB gadgets that you plug in, or something the dimensions of a floppy disk drive that you connect inside the case such that it pokes out at the front just like a disk drive. Other examples are the media displays that, like the front of a car stereo, show what's playing. They sit where a DVD drive would sit. Also available are temperature readers that show how hot your system is running – something practical for those who like their overclocking on the extreme side.

Essential tools for your PC

10

Introduction

With your PC set up for top performance you'll want to keep it that way and you'll also want to get the best software for it, without spending a fortune. Just because Windows comes with a few tools, it doesn't mean they're the best in their class, so take your pick from this selection of the best programs that all PC users should have. Quite a few of them are available free.

From useful utilities that will keep the system streamlined and protected from attack to those essential applications, this selection is the best software you can find on the net for immediate download. The software in this section is picked also for its slim-line installation. While the worst Windows applications are bloated with features you don't use and that eat up disk space and resources, those advocated here are trim and lean, helping to keep your PC flying.

Finding alternatives to Windows

There is alternative free software to most popular products you might otherwise buy, with OpenOffice.org helping huge numbers of users do office tasks for free. Indeed, this book was written using OpenOffice Writer. Why stop there, however? If you're feeling really brave you can do away with Windows altogether and try a version of the Linux operating system like Ubuntu, www.ubuntu.com or Red Hat, www.redhat.com.

These sites let you download the latest version of their operating systems that you then burn to CD-ROM and install either over or alongside Windows XP. Not only are they free but they offer many of the same features as Windows at none of the cost. Linux is also more secure, less prone to viruses and more reliable than Windows.

Don't pay a fortune for Microsoft Office when you can get a perfectly good equivalent for absolutely nothing. This package is freely downloadable and comprises a word processor, spreadsheet, database, drawing tool and presentation creator. All the files it creates are compatible with MS Office so you can take them into work or use them on other machines.

The programs all look and work almost identically to their Office equivalents but with fewer of the extravagant features that come with Office. There's no online research feature, for example, but it's hardly challenging to launch your web browser and do your research that way. All the essentials are there like spell checking and advanced formatting.

The OpenOffice.org project has been going since 2000 and is now a well established organisation with a high-quality application. The fact that the bundle is offered free to individuals and companies makes most people perk up, take notice and wonder what the catch is. To put your mind at rest, there isn't one. The only black mark against OpenOffice.org is that the formatting of some files may change slightly when opened up in MS Office. So check before you send any important work up to your boss. On the positive side, it can create PDF files and can be installed on as many machines as you like without concern regarding licenses. Just one note: make sure you download the latest stable release. There are later, under-development versions that you can get but its best to stick with the latest tried and tested version.

10

Working with OpenOffice.org

OpenOffice.org works and looks like most other office packages and is updated regularly. Best of all, it is free. So it's a very good candidate to be the first major program you install on your new PC. Once installed, you'll see six items in the start-menu folder. Base is the database application; it starts with a helpful wizard that lets you create a new database immediately and provides wizards to create forms, queries, tables and reports. Calc looks and works pretty much like Excel or any other spreadsheet and has equivalent features such as functions, goal seeking, charts and much more. Draw can be used to create vector and 3D graphics and is ideal for making little bits of art that you can use in presentations and documents. Impress is OpenOffice's version of PowerPoint and has probably the most obvious flaw in that it lacks the huge number of templates of the Microsoft program. However, you can rapidly download your own stock of them from a host of sites with a simple Internet search. Next up is Math, a formula creation tool, useful for scientists and students. It is packed with functions, operators and formulae and creates them as you'd see on a professor's chalkboard. Finally, Writer is just as good as Word and packed with many of the same features.

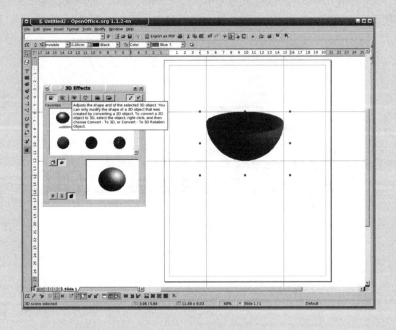

Freshly charged up to join in the re-invigorated battle of the browsers, Opera offers the usual latest features of a web browser. These include easily accessible tabs to enable you to have multiple pages open. It also remembers what you were looking at when you shut it down, so it'll open with the same pages open.

Apart from the built-in BitTorrent downloader, the best thing about Opera, one that makes it stand out from the crowd, is something very new in the form of its widgets. These are a collection of small programs that sit outside the browser window on your desktop and provide online information in a stylish and funky way. For example, the weather forecast for your town can appear in a smart little bubble, and sports results can appear on a ticker down the side. Individuals are encouraged to create and program their own widgets, so the potential is massive for these tiny programs to make a big impact on the desktop.

As browsers become the tool more of us use to access data they'll change radically over the next couple of years. While Opera isn't yet as popular as Internet Explorer or Firefox it is showing them both the way forward.

10

Browsing in Opera

▶

Opera has a host of features that you don't see in other browsers, thanks to its widgets that anyone can develop. To use them, go to the Widgets menu and choose Add widgets. Then browse through the pages that it shows and download the ones you want. Downloaded widgets will appear in the same menu and, to launch one. you just click on it.

Since widgets can cover almost any topic, they can be pretty much any shape or size from a nice narrow strip that you can place across the top of your desktop to something that takes up a fair amount of space. However, lots of widgets have different display modes so you can click a button for a nice narrow view and click again to change the widget window to see more detail.

1. Tabs – tabbed browsing is all the rage. It allows us to keep many websites open at the same time. Just what sites have you got open? Opera's useful preview feature means you just hold the mouse over a tab to see what lies inside.

2. Fast search – don't bother going to Google to do your searching, just type in what you're after here and you'll be taken directly to the results page.

3. Widgets – you can download individual widgets and put them anywhere you like on the desktop, with as many or as few as you want active at any one time.

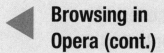
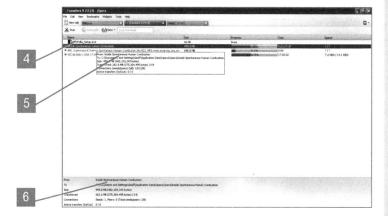

4 BitTorrent downloads are the future of downloading, unless you want to pay for a service. This distributed service means you're helping people get files as well as downloading them yourself. Whenever you click on a BitTorrent link in Opera it will start the download on this page.

5 Clicking on the BitTorrent tab shows up a list of files you are downloading, how fast they are downloading and an estimate of when they will be completed.

6 In the bottom section you can see the details for each file. Click on each one to find out about it and, most importantly, where the file will be stored finally.

10

Discovering Google Earth: www.google.com

If you're a bit bored with PCs and wonder what innovation there's been in the last few years then take a look at Google Earth. Not only can it show you a decent size image of your house and back garden, but it works as a mapping tool, a guide to local shops and services, as well as a brilliant desktop time waster.

Google Earth works because anyone can put information and links about anywhere on a web page that you can link into the program. From a global view to your own back yard you can zoom in from space to look at natural wonders or man-made structures large and small.

It has many and varied practical applications too: as a house-buying assistant, you can see aerial shots of any railway lines, sewage works or other nasties that might lurk around a potential property; as a route planner you can see in real images the possible journeys you might take; and, if you're studying, then it makes a useful geographical tool.

While some parts of the world, and even the more remotes parts of the UK, haven't been covered in high-definition photos yet, this is still worth a download so you can smoothly scale in from the heavens and do some curtain twitching from on high.

Google Earth gives you a fantastic eye on the planet from a whole-world view right down to your back garden. It is updated regularly, and downloads all the latest available satellite and aerial imagery from servers to improve its results and keep it up to date. The latest version has a smart new Earth control in the top right corner. With it you can zoom in and out, move around the face of the Earth, and angle the map. To find places directly, you can use the search box. As the project expands you'll be able to use the program for more and more map-based tasks. Some cities have 3D models of their major buildings and 3D terrain is being added so you can swoop through some major natural landmarks. Being an American-developed program, most of the new, cool stuff is on their continent but it should spread around the globe over time. For now, it's great fun just to play some of the many games that you can come up with. Examples include: finding crop circles around the world; detecting in-flight aircraft around the world's airports; tracking down natural wonders such as volcanoes; and finding man-made structures like the tallest buildings or massive dams.

Using Google Earth

1. Just type in a location in the Fly To box to head to a location; remember there are often a large number of places with the same name so you might have to pick from a list.

2. You can add your favourite places and arrange them into categories in this box.

3. A lot of information and detail is stored in the program, largely for the United States; it can be turned on or off here.

4. Use the central controller like a joystick to move the map around, the arcs to rotate it and the outer strips for tilt and zoom.

10

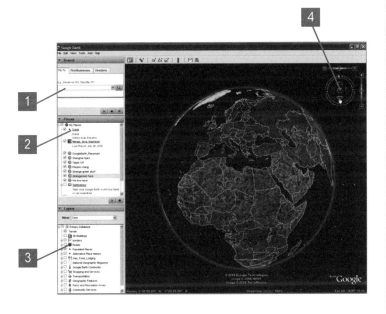

Using Google Earth (cont.)

5 The 3D-buildings feature adds a new dimension to maps. Hopefully, it will be expanded to other countries soon.

6 Roads and routes are available for most countries; they're provided on a neat overlay in distinctive colours.

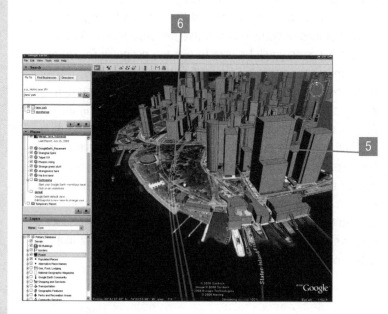

Entertaining with iTunes: www.itunes.com

Even if you don't have an Apple iPod music player, iTunes is still one of the smartest media players you can download. Available free, it opens up the world of podcasts, video and music downloads, all of which you can play on your PC. Using iTunes, you can download the latest movie trailers, films, TV episodes, as well as music at decent prices per track. Ideally you have an iPod to listen to these tunes on the go. There are ways around this though if you don't have one; just burn your iTunes tracks to CD and import them back, so you can convert them to play on any MP3 player.

Podcasts, if you're not familiar with the term, are audio recordings made by, well… anyone really. They're put up on the net in an episodic format for anyone to download. The most popular examples are created by professional media types, the likes of Ricky Gervais and Pete Tong for instance, and you can download these from the major radio stations. iTunes, though, has a great list of many popular ones. The real power of the podcast, however, is that anyone can create one, on any subject, and add it to the huge lists to which you can subscribe at no cost at all. So, if you want to listen to one about your favourite sports team, technology or pop star, there's more than likely one out there. If not, why not start one? There are plenty out there to download that cover PCs, overclocking and modding, as well as most other gadgets and hobbies.

iTunes also comes with QuickTime, Apple's video player and codec system. It's a required part of the install but is useful to have around anyway as a lot of official web movies come in this format.

10

Using iTunes ▶

1 The Library contains all of
your song tracks, including
those purchased online,
downloaded free, or copied
from your own CD.

2 In the Podcasts section you
can manage all the podcasts
you download. Once
subscribed, iTunes will get
them all for you automatically,
ready to play or copy to your
MP3 player.

3 Videos are a growing area of
iTunes. Movies and TV
episodes for download along
with music videos and
cartoons can be played on
your desktop or on a Video
iPod.

4 Playlists are the power behind
iTunes, allowing you to create
your own endless albums for
particular moods or
occasions.

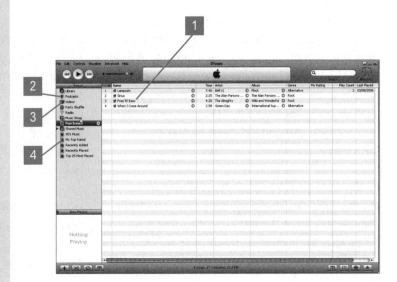

With luck, this program will have come supplied on one of your driver or program disks as it's the standard document-reading program for PCs. If not, then download it now and enter the world of the PDF file. Since paper manuals are going the way of the dodo, all your documentation is usually supplied in this way. The PDF will look the same on any PC and can be printed and managed with ease.

If you want to design and make your own PDF files then you can use the free tools that come with OpenOffice.org, covered earlier in this chapter. Or, you can invest in the full Adobe Acrobat program. Also, there are several tools that you can download that will help you make PDF files from your own documents in other programs, like Word for example. They are somewhat cheaper than Acrobat which is a professional creation application.

Almost any document can be turned into a PDF. It's an ideal form for sending a document in that people can read, but not change, your work. If you use your PC for business, then Acrobat Reader will be essential as most documents are disseminated this way.

10

Mailing with Eudora:
www.eudora.com

Outlook Express has long been derided as one of the least effective email programs available but, since it comes free with all XP systems, many don't complain or look for an alternative. Eudora is an example of an acceptable alternative that you can download. It comes in three versions. The Lite version is free, basic but functional and is a big improvement on Outlook Express. Sponsored Mode comes with a small advert in the corner and activates more features than are available on Lite. Paid Mode costs you money but opens up all Eudora features including SpamWatch, Ultra-fast searching and Bosswatch.

This last highlights any emails from important people in your life.

With Eudora you can handle multiple accounts, create neat folders for all your mail and flag up important messages for later action. Not only does it look better than Outlook Express and is easier to use, it has the reputation of being less vulnerable than Microsoft's program. While Microsoft has gone a long way to improve security with Outlook Express, it is still way behind the security level of a program with the reputation of Eudora Lite.

Anti Virus Guard performs the same services as other virus protection programs that you'd pay for but with the brilliant advantage that it is free. That's a big advantage in this field because most virus checkers come with a one-year subscription so you have to keep paying for them again and again.

With daily updates that can be installed automatically as soon as you switch on, you're protected against the latest threats. While it might not have the smartest interface or come in a

pretty box, that's never been the point of software that will prevent your data from being stolen or wiped out by a malicious program. Integrating well with Windows Security Center, AVG Free provides all the protection you need from modern threats with an ever-present shield, email scanner and virus vault.

AVG also offers a firewall program for your complete protection but, since Windows' own firewall seems to do a reasonable job, there is little need to complicate matters.

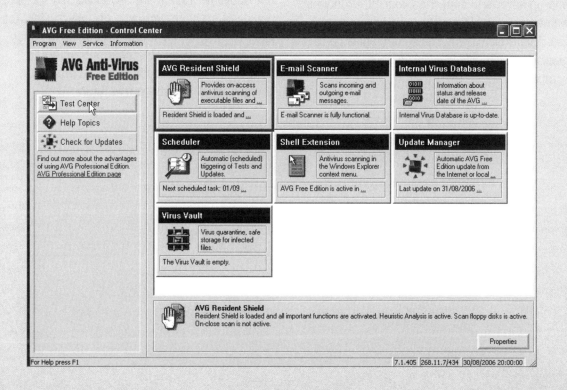

10

Preventing spyware with Stopzilla: www.stopzilla.com

This shareware program is one of the hottest around for detecting the menace of spyware on your system. Spyware is a malicious program, often hiding inside another file you may have installed or cunningly downloaded onto your computer through a bogus website. Spyware is so called because it can send information about you, your computer and what you do with it back to its creators. It can also leave back doors open on your PC for the creators to rifle through your files as well as cause damage on its own. One of the most common uses of spyware is to cause pop-up adverts to appear on your PC or in your web browser, replacing the adverts you should see. This explains why some companies go to great lengths to sneak spyware onto your computer.

StopZilla comes with a free 15-day trial and plenty of features to help keep spyware off your system. With a pop-up blocker to stop unwanted adverts and a black list to keep repeat offenders at bay, StopZilla offers double protection against some of the worst threats on the net. With spyware hiding almost anywhere and with its creators becoming increasingly clever at hiding it on your system, you can't really afford to be without some protection against it. There are dozens of anti-spyware programs out there but this one has a little personality to it that sees it rise above the rest. Many advanced users keep a couple of spyware programs on their system for extra security and if you use StopZilla together with the advanced scanning of a program like Spybot or Ad-Adware for complete protection, you're sure of a spyware-free future.

10

Jargon buster

Spyware – the term refers to any program that is installed on your PC without your consent, or one that is installed without explicitly telling you that it sends information, or explaining its purpose. Some spyware is benign, merely sending information about updates or technical issues. The worst kind, however, can fill your PC with unwanted advertising, tell its owner about what you do on your PC or steal files and personal information and send it to criminals.

Squashing files with WinZip: www.winzip.com

Windows XP was the first version of the operating system to come with some sort of built-in compression, but it's hardly a well-featured tool and you might not even notice it as you use the system. It makes it possible for Windows to use compressed files that are often called Zip files. But to make your own and manage these Zip files the easy way, you want to download something like WinZip. The program is officially shareware so you really should pay for it at some point. WinZip is ideal for squashing a host of related files together, keeping them in one neat file; and with password protection or data encryption if you need.

Using a friendly wizard, you can create new archives of your files. WinZip's features are also available in the context menu (right-click after selecting a range of files), so you don't even need to launch the program yourself. Advanced features include turning archives into .EXE files so people can run them on their own systems without WinZip; the archives are split so they will fit on a number of floppy disks or CD-ROMs depending on their size and your resources. You can also change the level of compression to keep file sizes really small or to be larger but open a little quicker.

There are other archiving programs available besides WinZip. Winrar is useful if you download files from newsgroups or torrents. The free and popular 7-Zip supports most of the common archive formats.

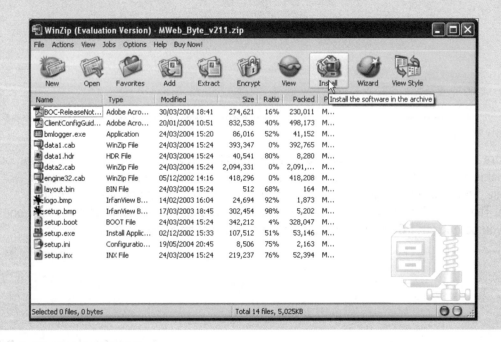

Solving hardware problems

Introduction

After all the fun of building your PC and installing Windows and the software to make it a truly useful machine, hopefully, you haven't come across any major problems. If you have, then these are the pages to turn to. They cover everything, well everything common or predictable, that can go wrong with the system.

Hardware problems come in three basic categories: something isn't plugged in correctly; something doesn't work; and something (software or driver) isn't installed properly. We'll tackle each scenario in turn and in the order they can happen after switching on your PC.

No system power

One of the worst feelings when using a computer is if you press the power button and nothing happens. All of a sudden you can't access your email and data, and you seem to have an expensive metal breeze block on your hands. When you turn a functional computer on you should hear the fans starting to rotate, a single beep from the case and then the monitor should come on. If you fail to observe any of these signs, the solution to this problem can be traced to a few physical objects, making it a simpler problem to solve than many.

While the advice here does sound like stating the obvious, we've all made this mistake at some point. The first thing to do is start at the end and check that the switch on the wall socket is on; and that of the extension lead if you're using one. Down the back of most PCs and behind the computer desk is a jungle of wires that can easily be turned off by moving feet, dropped objects and other seemingly innocuous actions. Check these for a firm fit.

Next, check that the switch on the power supply unit is also set to on. Now try the mains power switch again. If still nothing happens then it is

time to either swap the power lead for a different one or change the fuse if you don't have another lead. Most monitors and printers come with the usual kettle-plug style lead so you can do a quick change and try again to see if things work this time. If a different lead works then we can assume the fuse on the original lead has gone and it's time to get a replacement.

If there is still no life in the machine, it's time to take a peek inside. This is where those of us with Perspex sides to our cases have a bit of an advantage. Almost all motherboards these days have a LED on the board to indicate power is getting through. If you can see the light working then clearly we have power but nothing is happening with the computer. If there is no light on the motherboard even after you've changed the fuse (note that a PC power cable should be fitted with a 5-amp fuse), then it could be that the power supply unit has failed. These are rare occurrences but with tens of millions of PSUs running every day, some are statistically bound to fail and it does happen. The only solution to this problem is to get a replacement and see if that solves the problem.

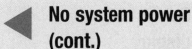

If you have a functioning one from your old PC then you can sit it on top of the case, replace the two internal connections from the non-functioning unit, and try it to see if that makes things better. If the old power supply unit works then we have identified the culprit. Your new PSU should be under warranty so it should be a straightforward job to get it replaced.

Important

Some power supply units are dual-region and will work on British 240 V or American/European 115 V mains power. These will have a switch on them, usually next to the power lead socket; ensure this is set to the 240 V setting.

11

Power but no display

In the normal course of starting up your PC, you hear the fans spin up and then a beep. The next thing that should happen is the monitor will come on and show the results of the POST test. If the screen doesn't light up then check the power lead as we did with the PSU to make sure that it works. Then check the cable connecting to the graphics card. These leads have small screws in the sides to lock them firmly in place but over time they can come loose. Also, if you don't use the screws in the first place then the lead is one nudge from falling loose out the back of the PC. If all is well with the cable and you still don't get a display then the graphics card is the likely culprit.

In the first instance check to see how many video connectors there are on it. If there happen to be two, as is the case with a lot of cards, switch the cable to the other plug and see if that sorts things out. The second issue might be that the video card isn't properly plugged into the slot. Even if it went in properly the first time, moving the PC to its final home can cause the odd instance of card-pop where it slides out of the slot enough to break the connection. This happens more often with people who upgrade a lot and don't bother to screw their cards firmly in place. Pop the side of the case off and inspect to ensure the card is fully in place. If it is, then turn the power on again and check that the fan on the graphics card is working.

Where there's power to the video card but still no display then it's most likely that something on the card is broken beyond our ability to fix it. If possible, try the monitor and the video card on another machine just to double check. In most of these cases you'll need to get a replacement card.

When your computer knows something is wrong, it doesn't tell you in English but with a series of beeps that can be deciphered with a look at the BIOS manual. The problem is, though, that most PCs don't come with manuals for the BIOS. This is a rather glaring error on the part of the PC industry but since it's rather rare for the BIOS to signal these errors, most of us will never notice.

When your computer does start beeping like an outraged R2-D2, you need to listen to the

number of beeps and note down the sequence. Then you'll have to find your BIOS type by looking at the screen where the computer usually stops when this kind of error occurs. The most common types are Award and AMI (American Megatrends). These days, most BIOS interfaces look roughly the same and have near identical features. In the next few years, however, we can expect smart programs to replace the old look of these interfaces.

For your information

Ami Error codes: If you have an AMI BIOS you can hear between 1 and 11 beeps. Refer to the table to find out the most likely suspect.

Number of beeps	Type of Error	Likely cause
1	Memory refresh	RAM
2	Memory parity error	RAM
3	Base memory failure	RAM
4	Timer not functioning	Motherboard
5	Processor error	CPU
6	A20 Gate failure	Motherboard or CPU
7	Processor exception	Processor
8	Video memory fault	Video card
9	ROM Checksum error	BIOS
10	CMOS checksum error	Motherboard
11	Cache memory failure	CPU or motherboard

11

When anything goes wrong with the hardware you need to listen and see what error the beeps correspond to. Check the connections for the offending component and, if possible, try a spare or replacement unit to see if that fixes the problem.

For your information

Award Error codes: Award BIOSes use different sounding beeps to attract your attention to a hardware problem

Number of beeps	Type of Error	Likely cause
1 Long 2 Short	Adapter failure	Video card
1 Long 3 Short	Adapter failure	Video card
Hi-low-hi-low beeps	CPU Failure	Processor
Hi beeps (while running)	CPU Overheat	Cooling
Repeating beeps	Memory failure	RAM

The mouse and keyboard are essential elements in using your PC so it becomes an extreme situation when one or both fail to work. For a start, if they both cease to function you cannot use your PC to solve the problem. Most input device problems are easily solved but it's always handy to keep an old-style PS-2 mouse and keyboard from a previous system in a cupboard, just in case something does go wrong; especially with any device that's battery powered or wireless.

The problem of a non-responding mouse or keyboard can be sorted quickly. First, check to

see if the cables are still firmly connected to the PC. Although it is rare for them to fall out, you never know. Next, you need to check and see if there are any lights working. Obviously, in the case of your rodent, this step only applies to optical mice. Everyone, however, can press the Caps Lock key to see if the function light changes on the keyboard.

More likely, one of the drivers has become corrupted or failed to load. If they are USB devices, the simplest test is to unplug the mouse and keyboard and plug them in again. Windows should spot them and reload the drivers. If they

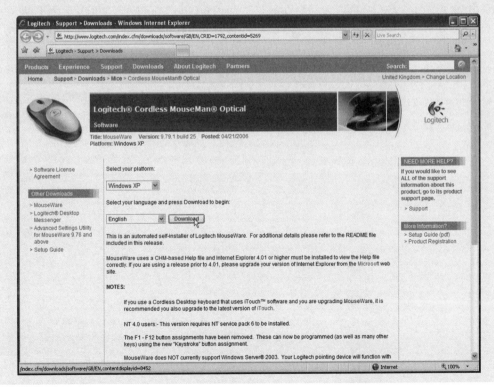

11

No mouse or keyboard function (cont.)

are PS-2 devices with round connectors then you will need to restart the computer to see if the PC will recognise them. This tip simply reactivates the existing driver but can often make a difference.

If it doesn't work, though, you'll need to download a new driver from the mouse and/or keyboard maker's site and install it to see if that fixes the problem. Microsoft and Logitech sell most mice and keyboards and their latest driver files are easily accessible on their sites. If yours isn't made by either company, you should track down the driver or use a generic one that comes with Windows. Uninstall any existing mouse or keyboard drivers before you install the new ones. Once these are working, your computer should

see the hardware again. If not, it's time to consider the possibility that something may have broken.

If the mouse or keyboard is battery powered, then replace the batteries or ensure they are fully charged. Make sure that none has leaked as this could have corroded the contacts. If there's still no joy then the last trick before declaring your peripheral dead is to try it on another computer. If they do work on a second system then the fact that they've packed up on one computer and work on another could just be one of the mysteries of computers. If you try different drivers, go back to a different System Restore or even go the whole hog and reinstall Windows; you can probably get them working again.

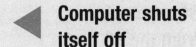

Computer shuts itself off

Sometimes your PC can seem to be working fine one minute and the next it suddenly switches off: i.e. it shuts down completely, as opposed to crashing and rebooting itself (a situation we'll cover further on in this chapter). While this is a rare fault, when it happens it can strike panic into the user. There is normally a rational explanation.

Should this problem occur, the first thing is not to panic or move. If there's a standby button on your keyboard, have you pressed it accidentally? This is common on laptops but is making an appearance on desktop keyboards too. If this is not the case, look at the power button on the case. By any chance has someone nudged the button? Computer cases under desks can be booted by a tapping foot and the power switch on the PSU can be tripped by objects falling down the back of a desk.

If neither of these seems to have caused the problem, then try turning the PC back on. If it rapidly switches off again then you may well have an overheating problem and need to check the connection between the CPU fan and the processor. On some systems you can hear a beeping warning as things get too hot to let you know this is happening.

Another reason for your computer shutting down may be that a loose connection from the power supply breaks the power link from time to time. Ensure all your cables are firmly plugged in. You might also want to check the power sections of your BIOS and in the Windows control panel; there may be a predetermined setting to shut it down after a period of time.

11

Strange noises from the PC

Your computer is an unlikely candidate for a haunting so there's usually a rational explanation for some strange sound emanating from inside the case. Here we cover the most likely suspects that can produce the oddest sounds from a system.

When you finished building your computer, the process of setting it up in its final place may have caused a few parts to move and shift ever so slightly. The most likely candidates to cause a noise are the cables, which could end up lying against one of the fans. This could produce anything from a little extra whir that you won't notice all the way up to a 'brrrr' sound that will soon get on your nerves. Solve this problem by just moving the cable out of the way or tie it to another cable to keep it firmly out of harm's reach.

Any distressed whirring or whining sound will probably be from a fan. It could happen immediately the PC is switched on or over time as a component warms up. PC fans are designed to be quiet and reliable but some, notably the cheaper ones, can wear out after a time or, because they're improperly built, will start

rubbing against something to cause a noise. The only solution with a dying fan is to get it replaced. Case or independent PSU fans are cheap and easy enough to replace but if it's in the power supply unit then you might need to replace the whole thing. A graphics card fan can sometimes be replaced. Recent video cards have heavily integrated cooling that might require a professional to replace it.

Other odd sounds can come from several sources. One of the most common is a dodgy CD or DVD in the drive. A severely scratched or a badly constructed and unbalanced disk can produce all manner of whirring or clicking noises in the drive. You'll know this is the case because the drive will be in use at the time. Floppy drives can also produce some alarming clicks, especially when the diskette is corrupt or scratched.

Saving the worst until last, the most uncomfortable sound coming from a PC will be a clicking or tick-tock noise that starts when your hard disk is being accessed. This means that the drive is more than likely beginning to fail and you need to backup your essential files as quickly as

Important

Ensure your computer is turned off when performing any kind of maintenance.

possible. Get it replaced under warranty or buy a new one. The sound is caused by the drive heads flicking around trying to access data. If they start hitting the drive surface then the drive can rapidly become unusable. Hard drives usually have three to five-year warranties and 'Between Mean Failure Times' rated in millions of hours. However, as prices have come down to make them just another upgrade, it seems their reliability has become slightly more fallible. Over a dozen years in PC computing I have seen drives fail every two years on average and any self-respecting IT department will have a nice stack of broken drives somewhere.

For your information

Keep your fans clean: As the fans are the parts that move the most in a PC it is they that will attract all the dust, hair and other grime that floats about in the household air. At least a couple of times a year, and more often if you notice lots of detritus building up, take the time to clean the fan vents, blades and surfaces. Dirt build-up will slow down fan speed, decrease its efficiency, and increase the temperature in the case. If a fan stops working then it can lead to the failure of more-expensive components so it pays to check.

The best weapon against grime and dust in the PC is air-in-a-can. You can get this from most technical stores such as Maplin. It blasts compressed air across the surface and, via a straw, into nooks and crannies to disturb the dust that can be vacuumed up by one of those neat little PC cleaners or your household vacuum cleaner, as long as you're very careful with the nozzle.

Blue-screen problems

1. Note that these problems may be a one-off occurrence, happen randomly over a long period of time or quite regularly, depending on the actual fault.

2. Follow the advice if it applies to your situation but if not then the best thing to do is restart Windows.

3. Windows will use this error code to check and see if the problem can be solved by the operating system.

The blue screen of death is a long-standing Windows tradition. It means that something has gone seriously enough wrong with your PC for Windows to cease functioning and crash. The blue screen you see as this happens usually has an error message pointing to the cause. Either hardware or software problems, or a combination of both, can cause these rare but alarming errors.

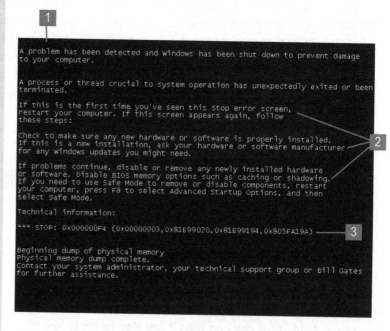

When one of these errors occurs the first thing you should do is restart the computer. If it keeps running after the reboot, you will be given a chance to report the fault. If you let it do this, and it is worth the effort, the feature will check against Microsoft's error database and see if there's a solution to the problem.

Hopefully Windows will either fix the problem or guide you closer to the culprit. If you consistently see blue screen errors with the same problem then anything from defective RAM to a failing hard drive could be causing it and whatever it is will need replacing.

**Blue-screen
problems (cont.)**

Jargon buster

Blue Screen of Death – the popular name for a system error that brings the computer to a halt. There are a range of errors that can cause this situation, producing the infamous blue screen along with a technical error message. Some blue screens can be overcome by waiting but, in most cases, a restart is required. If the blue screen is repeated often for the same program then it should be uninstalled, patched or reinstalled. If the same error-screen is seen over a range of different situations then a problem could exist with your hardware or Windows XP's own files.

11

Solving hardware problems 179

Maintaining your computer

Introduction

So you've fought your way past any hardware troubles, now all that can go amiss is Windows itself. While Windows XP is a lot less frail than its predecessors, there is still a lot that can go wrong and leave you cursing your otherwise shiny, new PC. But it does have several useful free tools that will help keep your computer clean and running smoothly.

What you'll do

Recover disk space

Defragment your hard disk

Create scheduled tasks

Mission accomplished

Recovering disk space

1. Disk Cleanup takes a few minutes to analyse your hard drive and tell you what it can do to help improve performance.

2. Disk Defragmenter can be launched from here or as part of Disk Cleanup. It reorganises your files for faster access.

3. Use Scheduled Tasks to organise regular clean-ups of your system. It's all too easy to forget, so automating the process will help keep your system running.

The first thing you'll notice about a new Windows XP installation is how fast everything runs in comparison to using a well-used system full of programs and clutter. Keeping it that way is, rather like staying on a diet, a matter of willpower. Thankfully Windows has a few tools to help keep the gradual slowdown in check; that's half the problem really. The system's speed bleeds away so slowly that you don't notice until you next get your hands on a fresh PC.

You can find those handy free PC utilities in the System Tools folder inside the Accessories menu item on the Start Bar. In the list, the first of these is Disk Cleanup, which helps to free up disk space. This is something that even the largest drive will find in increasing demand as time passes. Its close cousin Disk Defragmenter is used to arrange the files in a neater order and to stitch back together files split across the drive, for faster performance. You should also make use of Scheduled Tasks to add a degree of order to your housekeeping regime.

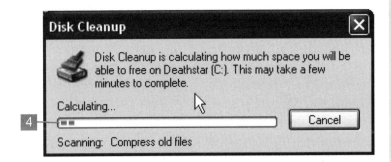

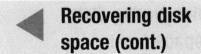

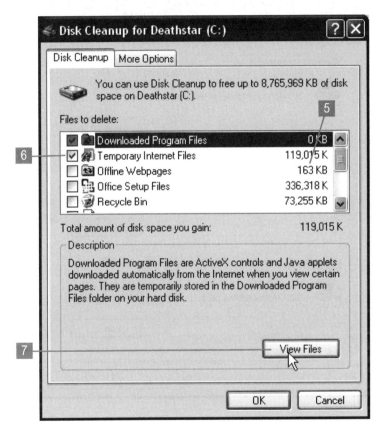

4 Launch Disk Cleanup and it will check through your hard disk for areas where it can help you recover wasted disk space.

5 On the Disk Cleanup tab you can see where disk space is being potentially wasted.

6 Tick the boxes that you are happy to see deleted or compressed to save space, then click OK to start what can be a long process depending on the amount of space to be saved.

7 If you want to be sure about what you're deleting click on the View Files button to inspect the contents of each area you want to delete.

12

8 On the More Options tab, you can free up more space by deleting some programs or files that aren't used.

9 The Windows Components pane lists all the parts of Windows that you have installed, many of which you don't use so can happily delete.

10 Installed Programs takes you to part of the Control Panel (where it's called Add or Remove Programs) and lets you remove applications you don't use anymore to free up disk space.

11 If you keep making regular System Restore points then the old ones are likely to be out of date and can be removed.

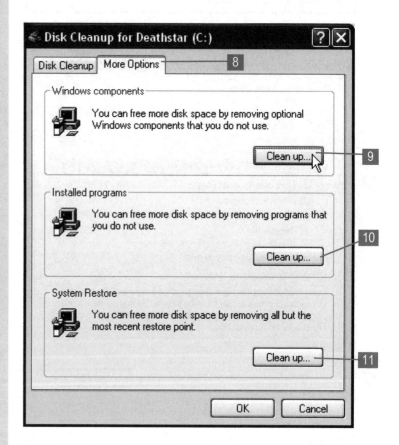

Recovering disk space (cont.)

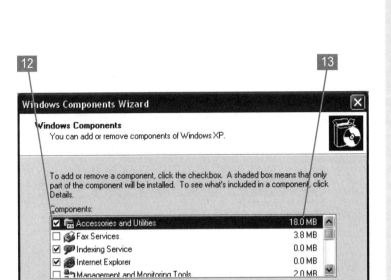

12 Tick those services you want to delete, something like Fax Services is redundant on most PCs.

13 You can see how much disk space you'll be saving on the left; some take up no space so aren't worth worrying about.

14 Highlight one component and click Details to see more about what you'll be removing, you can also choose to remove some parts of a single component.

15 Click Next when you've chosen what you want to delete and are sure you won't need it.

12

16 The four tabs down the left-hand side help you manage adding, removing and changing Windows programs.

17 Choose a program you want to delete; you can sort the list by size to find out the worst offending space-hogs.

18 Click on the Remove button to get rid of the program and recover some of that valuable disk space.

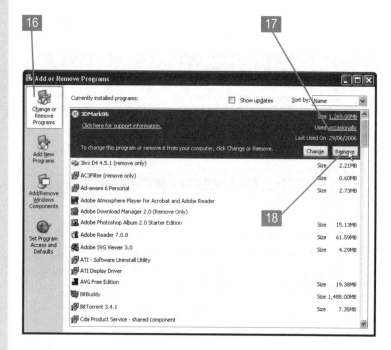

With a new hard drive offering lots of room, programs are installed in a nice, neat order over the surface of the disk. As it fills up, larger files have to be split up across the drive forcing the drive to take longer to load them. When this starts happening to smaller files, your disk can be considered to be highly fragmented and you'll notice that many tasks take longer to start because of the extended loading times. Defragmenting used to be a religious part of PC maintenance in the days of smaller hard drives and shouldn't be overlooked just because we all have huge amounts of storage. We tend to ignore the fact that games and applications take up far more room than they used to, so it all fills up just the same.

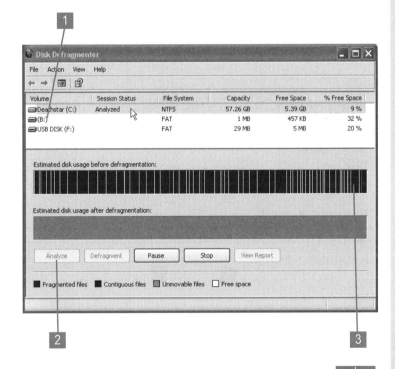

1   When you launch Disk Defragmenter you will see all your drives displayed, these can include floppy disks, memory cards, drive partitions and other storage.

2   Choose your hard drive from the list and click on Analyze. It'll take a minute to scan your hard disk for its level of fragmentation.

3   The striped line across the window shows how badly broken up the files are on the drive. On a new drive there would be large blocks of the same colour indicating that files are neatly arranged.

Important

Defragmenting needs at least 15 % of your disk space free to be able to work efficiently. It can work with less but will take longer to complete, so it's wise to use Disk Cleanup and get rid of any other large files you don't need before starting Disk Defragmenter.

Jargon buster

Defragmenting – once your hard disk begins to run out of room, it will start splitting large files up and putting them in the small gaps left between other files. These take longer to find and read because the drive has more work to do. Defragmenting the drive means the program will sort all the files back into a sensible order.

12

Defragmenting your hard disk (cont.)

[4] Once the analysis is complete, you are advised either to not bother defragmenting the drive or to let the computer sort it out.

[5] To see more details click on View Report and you'll be shown detailed information about the scan.

[6] If you don't want to read the report, click Defragment to start the long process. Make sure you read our Timesaver tip before you start!

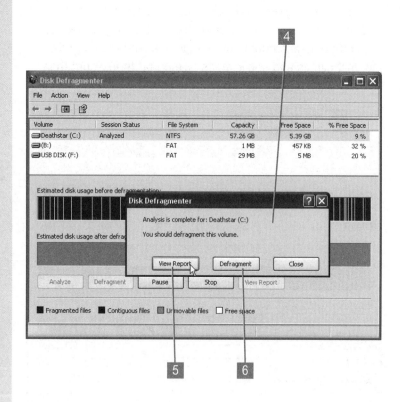

Timesaver tip

Defragmenting requires your PC to be doing nothing that will change the state of the hard drive as the utility works. Given that it can take a good hour or longer to work its magic, you don't want to do this more than once during your clean up. If some process or program that will change the state of the hard disk is running then the defrag will stop and have to restart from the beginning. To save a lot of time, make sure that all other programs are closed including anything non-essential in the background. Ensure that screensavers are disabled and all Internet programs are turned off. Keep an eye on the defrag for the first five minutes to make sure it doesn't restart; thereafter you should be fine to let it run! The full process can take a couple of hours.

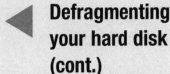

Defragmenting your hard disk (cont.)

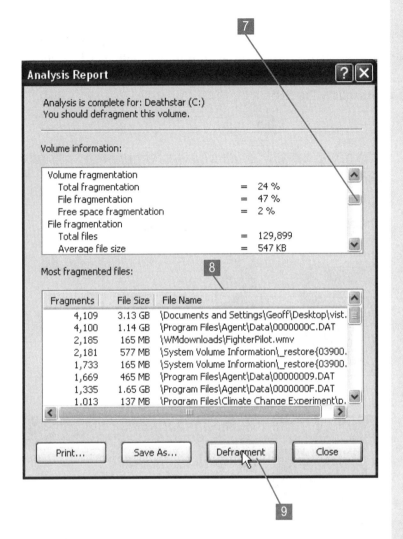

7 If you asked to view the report you go to this screen. Scroll down the Volume Information list and you'll see the percentage of fragmentation on your drive along with more detailed data on the files.

8 The Most Fragmented Files list shows which files are the worst culprits. Try to use any of these files before and after you've tidied the drive and you might detect the time saved in loading them.

9 Click Defragment to start the long process. Make sure you read our Timesaver tip before you start.

Jargon buster

Screensaver – so called because they were originally used to prevent screens being damaged by individual characters remaining too long in the same place on the screen when the system was left alone. Nowadays they are more decorative affairs and range from simple image slideshows to impressive 3D animations, the most popular being a life-like fish tank. They can prevent people seeing what's on your screen and can be password protected to stop people using your machine when you are absent. When defragmenting or doing other intensive work they can confuse the system, so should be disabled at such times.

Creating scheduled tasks

The Scheduled Tasks utility allows you to run programs on a regular basis, allowing us forgetful humans to not have to worry about running those essential cleaning programs. It uses a neat wizard to help you choose the program and the times you want it to run. Scheduled Tasks can also be chosen to run any program, so you can set up your own automated backups and save having to splash out on a program that does essentially the same.

1 When you launch Scheduled Tasks it might be largely empty, or a few items might have been placed there depending on the software you have installed. What you'll definitely see is the Add Scheduled Task option. Click on this.

2 You'll see this wizard; click Next to start. It'll take a few seconds to find all your executable programs that you might choose in creating a task.

3 From the list, search out the program you wish to create a task for. Disk Cleanup is present on this computer.

4 If you can't see a program you want to use then click the Browse button and locate the file manually.

5 Then click Next to move to the next stage.

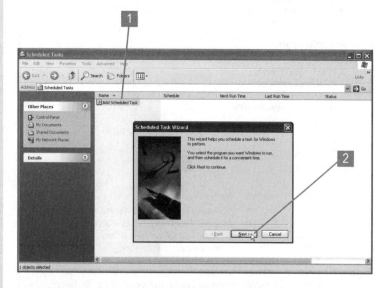

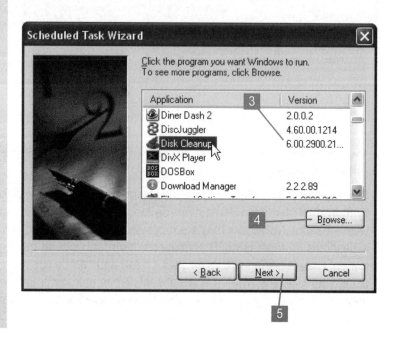

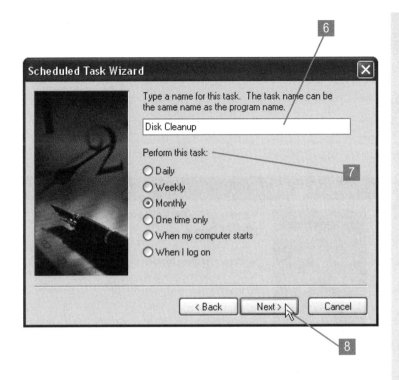

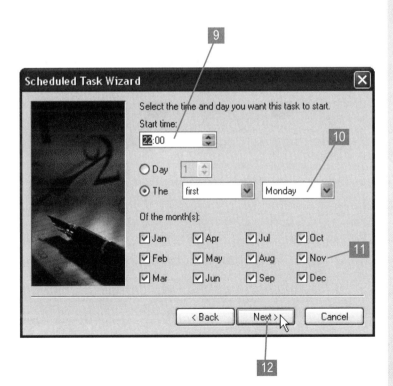

Creating scheduled tasks (cont.)

6 If you have lots of tasks running then you'll want to give them meaningful names here but for now we don't really need to change this title.

7 Choose the frequency with which this task will be performed. For something like disk maintenance once a month is probably more than enough.

8 Click Next to set the scheduling.

9 Select a start time for your task. With something that takes as long as disk defragmentation you might want to make it at the end of the day and leave the computer running overnight.

10 Choose what day you want your task to start. Your options are highly flexible so choose what best suits your computer usage patterns.

11 Pick which months you want it to run. Obviously, if you only want this to occur on a quarterly basis then de-list the unneeded ones.

12 Click Next to check the instruction.

12

Maintaining your computer 191

Creating scheduled tasks (cont.)

13 If you want to fiddle with the task details then tick Open Advanced Properties.

14 Click Finish to complete the task. Repeat the process for any others you want to launch.

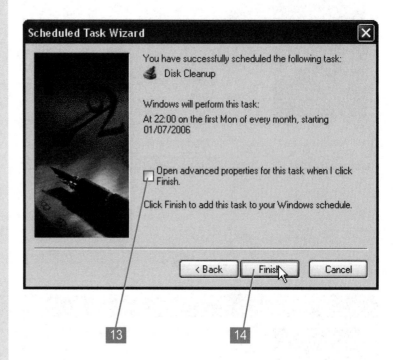

Scheduled Task Wizard

You have successfully scheduled the following task:

Disk Cleanup

Windows will perform this task:

At 22:00 on the first Mon of every month, starting 01/07/2006

☐ Open advanced properties for this task when I click Finish.

Click Finish to add this task to your Windows schedule.

< Back   Finish   Cancel

13   14

Mission accomplished

With this final chapter you now know all you need to help you choose the parts, build and test your own PC, find out how it can be improved and keep it running at its best. Hopefully, you will also start looking at your computer as a rather cunning whole; greater than the sum of its parts. You can appreciate how everything works together and know what to do when something goes wrong. Building your own PC now shouldn't look like some mountain to be climbed with only a small screwdriver to hand. It is a logical sequence of steps that will remain roughly the same no matter what new technologies are thrust into our hands in future. Processors will get faster, motherboards smarter and graphics more impressive but nothing about these developments should frighten the confident PC builder. Enjoy your new-found skills and we hope they bring you much enjoyment for a long, long time.

Jargon buster

BitTorrent – peer-to-peer file sharing that allows your computer to grab parts of a file from any computer that has it, and is sharing it. Thus, when thousands of people try to get a file at once, this load is taken off a single server and distributed around the web. You need to download a BitTorrent client before you can receive files in this way, try www.bittorrent.com/download.html/

Blue Screen of Death – the popular name for a system error that brings the computer to a halt. There are a range of errors that can cause this situation, producing the infamous blue screen along with a technical error message. Some blue screens can be overcome by waiting but, in most cases, a restart is required. If the blue screen is repeated often for the same program then it should be uninstalled, patched or reinstalled. If the same error-screen is seen over a range of different situations then a problem could exist with your hardware or Windows XP's own files.

DDR RAM – most motherboards use the cheap and plentiful DDR memory type while a few of the more expensive models will accept the higher priced RD-RAM. These two types of memory stick offer technically different philosophies on how memory and the computer should work together. To the layman, this is an irrelevance. Since DDR is a lot cheaper, the vast majority of users will go for motherboards that support that standard.

Defragmenting – once your hard disk begins to run out of room, it will start splitting up large files and putting them in the small gaps left between other files. These take longer to find and read because the drive has more work to do. Defragmenting the drive means the program will sort all the files back into a sensible order.

Driver – a piece of code that describes what your hardware can do and tells the PC and windows how to talk to it. Drivers can also include their own programs so you can enable features and adjust settings on that item of hardware.

Driver Signing – a signed driver is one that has been approved by Microsoft for use with Windows XP. This means that it has gone through all their quality checks. New drivers often aren't signed because it can take months for one to be checked, so don't worry if you get messages saying that your driver isn't signed. It is more a political statement as the majority of hardware companies do plenty of testing to ensure their driver works properly.

Dual-channel memory – memory makers have invented many tricks to make memory access faster. Dual channel is the latest of these. It allows the processor to talk to both banks of memory at the same time. To achieve this trick, the two sticks of memory have to be exactly the same type, called a matched pair, because the timing of communication between them and the processor is critical.

Dual-core – in an attempt to speed up computers in the past, motherboard makers put two processor slots on a single board. This was expensive and required lots of extra wiring. To cheapen the idea of doubling your power, Intel and AMD are both putting two, and now four, processor cores on a single chip, saving the motherboard makers doing any extra work. With two processors working together, tasks take less time and more work can be done between the cores.

eBay – the first online selling and buying site, eBay allows millions of us to put up for online auction, or sale at a fixed price, our unwanted possessions. eBay is so successful that many small businesses have started up selling PC parts and peripherals online, often far cheaper than you will find on the high street.

FAT – File Allocation Table refers to the old way Windows stored details about files and folders. Windows 95 used a 16-bit version called FAT-16 while 98 started using FAT-32 which doubled the amount of hard drive space that Windows could read.

Footprint – refers to the amount of space a PC case takes up. Cases are designed with the width of the CD/DVD drive and height of the motherboard in mind.

Heatsink – this specially designed metal construction is used to absorb heat from the processor. The heat is then dispersed by the fan to prevent the chip from overheating. A modern processor can run at up to 50–60 °C happily; any higher and you might want better cooling to prevent problems.

Intel Corp. – the organisation that invented the microprocessor has long been famous for creating the motherboards, chipsets and processors that lie behind the modern PC. Today, though, there are many different makers of components all of whom maintain compatibility with Intel's standards thereby allowing all PCs to run the same software and work together.

Linux – an operating system that is very different to Windows, Linux is based around industrial strength code that is less likely to crash but more complicated to manage. Modern Linux has a similar graphical interface for Windows but underneath is still a command-based language with many commands and parameters that have to be learnt.

Modders – describes PC enthusiasts who, while often interested in speed, are really into making their idea of the best looking PC. Some modded systems are truly things of beauty and design while others are just mad collections of neon lights. Some modders spend many times the value of a basic PC on a custom or homebuilt case and accessories.

NTFS – the New Technology File System is actually decades old and is a better-organised version of the FAT file system that Windows 98 and its predecessors used to employ.

OEM – stands for Other End Manufacturer and refers to individual computer parts that were intended to be bought by commercial PC builders for installing in the machines that they sell complete under their own brand name. Many of these parts, from processors to graphics cards, end up for sale to the public cheaper than the retail versions. The drawback is that often the warranty is shorter than that of the retail product and the part comes with none of the frills that you'd find in a retail box. So there's no fancy packaging, no extra software and the minimum of documentation.

Overclocking – refers to the technique of changing the speed of your CPU, graphics chip or memory to improve computer performance. This is possible because the actual speed of every chip made is slightly different. They are put together by approximate speed rating and marketed as running at a particular rate. However, the speed of each chip can be increased a little, or a lot, by changing BIOS settings or installing special software.

Pins – each pin on a processor is the physical connection to a data wire on the motherboard that links the processor to the other parts of the system.

Port – your computer accesses different Internet services through thousands of possible port numbers. A lot of these are blocked off to prevent hackers using them to gain access to your machine. If you want to make one specific port useable, you need to change the firewall to permit traffic on that port number.

POST – Power On Self Test is a series of checks the computer carries out on itself to ensure all is well with the main hardware components.

Power upgraders – what might start out as a couple of little tweaks can rapidly develop into a full blown hobby. Power upgraders live on the cutting edge of PC technology, always buying the latest and fastest gear, which they overclock to the maximum speed, to keep their PC running as fast as possible.

Product code – most programs come with a product or license code. Without it you cannot complete the installation of your program. It is vital, therefore, that you take care not to lose the manual or disk case if this has the number printed on it. With Windows you will need to activate the program within 30 days of installation, either online or over the phone. This checks that your license is genuine.

RAID – Redundant Array of Inexpensive Drives is a fancy way of saying that if you install two or more hard drives in your PC then you can back up your data between them. Therefore, if one file becomes corrupted you will always have a backup on one of the other drives. RAID does this automatically, so you need never worry about corrupt files again.

SATA – Serial Advanced Technology Attachment is a recent standard for connecting hard drives into computer systems. It was developed to speed up the way data is passed from the hard disk drive to computer memory. With a theoretical transfer rate of 150 megabytes per second, in reality it is barely faster than old EIDE drives. New, faster standards are promised. The real benefit, though, is in the thinner, more flexible cabling that saves space and is easier to install than the cabling of past drive technologies.

Screensaver – so called because they were originally used to prevent screens being damaged by individual characters remaining too long in the same place on the screen when the system was left alone. Nowadays they are more decorative affairs and range from simple image slideshows to impressive 3D animations, the most popular being a life-like fish tank. They can prevent people seeing what's on your screen and can be password protected to stop people using your machine when you are absent. When defragmenting or doing other intensive work they can confuse the system, so should be disabled at such times.

Spyware – refers to any program that is installed on your PC without your consent, or one that is installed without explicitly telling you that it sends information, or explaining its purpose. Some spyware is benign, merely sending information about updates or technical issues. The worst kind, however, can fill your PC with unwanted advertising, tell its owner about what you do on your PC or steal files and personal information and send it to criminals.

Thermal Paste – is a chemical compound, usually including silicon, silver or another metal that has good thermal properties, used to lift heat from the processor and pass it up to the cooling block and fan. It fills in the small dents and imperfections between the metals to aid conductivity.

Wi-Fi – is a standard set of protocols that allow computers to talk using radio waves. In the home, this is ideal for sharing an Internet connection between computers in different rooms. WiFi hotspots in public places such as designated coffee shops and libraries allow anyone using a laptop to access the Internet without worrying about plugging in or changing complicated settings.

Windows Registry – the power behind Windows is all in the Registry, a massive file that lists every piece of hardware and every system setting. It is read when the system starts up. Quite a few settings are worth changing to improve your system and improve stability. Over time, the registry can become clogged with old data, missing links and other errors that add to boot-up times and reduce system performance.

Troubleshooting guide

Security

Software

Windows